Ancestral Voices

Ancestral Voices

Reflections on Vedic, Classical and Bhakti Poetry

RAMESH CHANDRA SHAH

Foreword by
KATHLEEN RAINE

MOTILAL BANARSIDASS PUBLISHERS
PRIVATE LIMITED • DELHI

First Indian Edition: Delhi, 2006
First published in 2001 by
The Temenos Academy, U.K.

ISBN: 81-208-3054-7

Also available at:

MOTILAL BANARSIDASS
41 U.A. Bungalow Road, Jawahar Nagar, Delhi 110 007
8 Mahalaxmi Chamber, 22 Bhulabhai Desai Road, Mumbai 400 026
203 Royapettah High Road, Mylapore, Chennai 600 004
236, 9th Main III Block, Jayanagar, Bangalore 560 011
Sanas Plaza, 1302 Baji Rao Road, Pune 411 002
8 Camac Street, Kolkata 700 017
Ashok Rajpath, Patna 800 004
Chowk, Varanasi 221 001

PRINTED IN INDIA

BY JAINENDRA PRAKASH JAIN AT SHRI JAINENDRA PRESS,
A-45 NARAINA, PHASE-I, NEW DELHI 110 028
AND PUBLISHED BY NARENDRA PRAKASH JAIN FOR
MOTILAL BANARSIDASS PUBLISHERS PRIVATE LIMITED,
BUNGALOW ROAD, DELHI 110 007

For Somraj Gupta

who reveals the Word within the word

Contents

The Founding of Truth: Some Reflections on Vedic Poetry	2
Ancestral Voices in the Post-Vedic and the Classical Ages of Sanskrit Poetry	24
Towards a Philosophy of Imagination: Hints from Indian Aesthetics	44
Bhakti Poetry : Background and Perspective	62

Foreword

Western critics whose premisses are mainly secular, necessarily fail to understand the work and thought of a poet (W. B. Yeats) who throughout his life held a different view of reality, of which what passes for 'knowledge' in modern Western Universities is ignorant. The same spiritual and imaginative illiteracy applies of course to our reading of poetry as such, and it came as no surprise to me when I found the question formulated in a paper on Yeats and Eliot written in 1997 by Professor Ramesh Chandra Shah: 'Has the traditionally valid expectation of a special and indispensable kind of wisdom from poets become untenable in today's cosmopolitan civilisation?' I met Professor Shah at a conference at the India International Centre in Delhi, held jointly with the Temenos Academy, following which we invited him to lecture for us at the Temenos Academy in London in the summer of 1998. The time has come to re-learn from the Orient—and above all from the spiritual mainstream of India—that special kind of wisdom of which Professor Shah speaks.

It was to this mainstream that Yeats himself arrived in the course of his lifelong pursuit of the 'learning of the Imagination', and to which he offers us the guidance of his own studies and his beautiful translations of the Ten Principal Upanishads. If Yeats represents a turning-point of western imaginative literacy, Professor Shah's is a voice to which we are bound to listen.

—KATHLEEN RAINE

The Founding of Truth :

"What is for us imperceptible was for the ancients perceptible; thus it is recorded that Vyāsa and others used to meet the gods and ṛṣis face to façe...We do not have the right to measure by our capabilities the capabiltty of the ṛṣis who see the mantras and the Brahmanas."

—Śaṅkara (commentary on the Brahmasutra)

Our age has shifted all emphasis to the here and now and thus brought about a daemonization of man and his world. The phenomenon of dictators and all the misery they have wrought springs from the fact that man has been robbed of transcendence by the short-sightedness of super intellectuals. Like them he has fallen a victim to unconsciousness. But man's task is the exact opposite: to become conscious of the contents that press upward from the unconscious. Neither should he persist in his unconsciousness, nor remain identical with the unconscious elements of his being, thus evading his destiny, which is to create more and more consciousness. As far as we can discern, the sole purpose of human existence is to kindle a light in the darkness of mere being. It may even be assumed that just as the unconscious affects us, so the increase in our consciousness affects the unconscious.

—C.G. Jung: Memories, Dreams, Reflections, p. 326

Some Reflection on Vedic Poetry

I

If 'the nature of poetry', as Martin Heidegger says, is 'the founding of truth'[1], the Vedas may legitimately be considered to embody and enact this nature and, hence, to deserve not only our scholastic curiosity but some sort of an existential reenactment too. They are, after all, primordially spoken language—a set of words with meaning, sound and power. They have been preserved through millennia not as historical records, but as a revelation claiming perennial validity. If Carl Jung in the passage quoted above envisages the destiny of man as 'creating more and more consciousness', the Vedic poets seem to have made this destiny of man the foundational concern of their civilisational adventure. The Vedic revelation does appear to unfold the process of man's becoming conscious, of discovering himself along with the three worlds and their mutual relationships. Vāc, the Word is not just a man-made invention or a mere tool of communication. She is the primordial mystery combining in herself three worlds of time: past, present and future. There is a hymn in the *Ṛg Veda* addressed to Bṛhaspati, the inspirer of sacred poetry. The Word, it tells us originates from the seers and this revelation is achieved by love and active collaboration.

> O Lord of the Holy Word! That was the first
> Beginning of the Word when the seers fell to
> naming each object
> That which was best and purest, deeply hidden

1. *Poetry, Language, Thought*, Martin Heidegger, p. 75 (Trans. By Albert Hofstadter).

> Within their hearts, they revealed by the power of their love
>
> The seers fashioned the Word by means of their mind
> Sifting it as with sieves the corn is sifted
> Thus friends may recognize each other's friendship
> An auspicious seal upon their word is set.[2]

It is not to everyone that the Word reveals herself, but only to the one who is Worthy to receive her:

> Yet certain ones, though seeing, may not see her
> and other ones, though hearing may not hear her.
> But to some the Word reveals herself quite freely
> Like fair-robed bride surrendering to her husband.[3]

Only those who are endowed with depth can really hear the word; only through proper participation in the sacrifice can the strong thread be woven that holds together all the threads of the universe. 'Being ignorant they weave a faulty thread'—the hymn tells us. It is like a sacred competition: different roles are assigned to the participants: creation of poetry corresponding to the *Ṛg Veda*, melodious recitation corresponding to the *Sāma Veda*, exposition of its meaning is the part of the *Atharva Veda* and its application in the sacrifice is assigned to the *Yajur Veda*. Thus,

> One man with utmost care creates the verses;
> another signs a song in chanted meters.
> A third, the Brāhmin, tells the wisdom of being
> While yet a fourth prescribes the rules of sacrifice."[4]

---

2. *The Vedic Experience*, Tr. and commentary by Raimundo Panikkar, p. 94.
3. Ibid.
4. Ibid.

The metaphor of the thread or of weaving as such is quite common in the Vedas and yet it is literal too. Etymologically, a text is a piece of cloth; *textus*, from which the word derives, means woven. Thus it won't be irrelevant to mention the fact that here in the text of *Ṛg Veda*, the very notion of 'text' is for the first time given by the seer-poets who composed these hymns. They are aware not only that they are weaving a fabric, but that in this process the subject disappears in favour of the fire burning within him. Addressing this fire that resides in the heart, the *ṛṣi* exclaims, "I do not know how to stretch the thread and weave the cloth; But the Fire knows and it is he who will speak the appropriate words; for he is the immortal light within mortals, the one source of all thought." Elsewhere we hear another *ṛṣi* praying to Varuṇa, 'May we attain the fountain-head of the Truth that you guard. Do not let the thread break while I am still weaving this thought." In fact it is the ritual-offering of this fabric of words to the gods which constitutes the sacrifice: it is conceived by these poets as a text woven out of seven threads.' A hymn describing the primordial creation of sacrifice by the Cosmic Puruṣa (the primordial Man) says;

> "The sacrifice that is spread out with threads on all sides, drawn tight with a hundred and one divine acts, is woven by the fathers as they come near: 'Weave forward, weave backward' they say as they sit by the loom that is stretched tight. The Cosmic Man stretches the warp and draws the weft; the Man has spread it out upon the dome of the sky. That was the model for the human sages, our fathers, when the primeval sacrifice was born. With the eyes of my mind, I see those who were the first to offer the sacrifice."[5]

Every part of the Veda, if properly understood throws light upon every other part. Śri Aurobindo, who approached the

5. 'The *Ṛg Veda*: Text and Interpretation' in *Philosophy & Religion*, J.L. Mehta, p. 275.

Veda after a close study of the *Bhagavad Gītā* and the Upaniṣads and after having achieved mastery of the art of silencing the mind has rightly observed in one of his early essays that "the hymns of the *Ṛg Veda* always confirm each other by the same terms and ideas and the same relations of ideas." Thus the import of the hymn mentioned above becomes clearer when we remember parallel texts in *Atharva Veda*, and in *Ṛg Veda* itself that speak of two maidens, symbolizing Day and Night, dancing in circles and endlessly weaving the stuff of the world, spreading all the colours of reality over the six regions of the universe. Not only the cosmic forces but men and their ancestors also participate in this world-building. The rituals are the threads, the hymns the shuttles, the weavers the sacrifices. One of the Upaniṣads tells us that the gods were afraid of death and that each one covered himself with his respective meter to protect himself. That idea originated here in this hymn, where each god has his own meter in which he is praised and which strengthens him. The poets themselves are left wondering whether it is the gods who are behind their songs or their poetry that vivifies the gods :

> The Gāyatrī metre became the yokefellow of Agni
> Savitṛ took as his companion the meter Uṣṇih
> Soma, the one who is praised by hymns took
> anuṣṭubha
> While the word of the Lord of speech was
> strengthened by Bṛhatī.[6]

So this is perhaps the most characteristic feature of the Vedic vision and experience of life: this notion of weaving a fabric in words, a gift of the gods to man and rendered back to them, in thankfulness and as a token of mutuality, in the service of Truth which the gods themselves serve. It is necessary to pinpoint and emphasize this—the sustaining power of his vision of the relationship between word and man in our

6. A hymn from the *Ṛg Veda*, tr. by R. Panikkar in *The Vedic Experience.*

religious history, which even in later times of ritualistic extravagance was never quite lost sight of.

II

The present form of the hymns appears to draw upon a more ancient tradition of myths which is fragmentarily embedded in them. Mythically expressed vision of the ancient seers, ritualistic systematization and symbolism of the priests and the cognitive enquiry of the sages—these then would appear to be the three broad stages through which the development of Vedic life and sensibility has passed. The most widely current assumption in modern scholarship about Vedic religion is that it represents a primitive and polytheistic nature-worship which was followed by speculative monism on the one hand and magical ritualism on the other. But almost all the famous modern Indian scholars, religious leaders and sages like Dayānanda Saraswatī, Śrī Aurobindo, Anirvāṇa and Āṇanda Coomāraswāmy have refuted this assumption through their own readings and interpretations of the hymns. For all of them, however, the Vedas are the primary source of knowledge about their meaning and in this respect they all are attuned to modern critical scholarship. Unfortunately, the dominant schools of Indological scholarship have been hampered by ideological and methodological prejudices of one sort or another. It is seldom recognised that inspite of the most dramatic changes and ruptures in their religious history, the one thing to which Hindus clung and tenaciously held on by dint of continued creative transformation, was their immediate, living relationship with the sacred, articulated in diverse ways from time to time in response to the challenge and crisis they faced. But instead of the urge to go deep into the secret of this inner resilence, western scholarship has mostly been content to represent it as a failure to rise above primitive animism, a failure to move from magic to reason or from reason to faith. The discipline of modern anthropology too has hardly helped to loosen the grip of this ideological fixation, because it has been built upon a rationalistic—positivistic and evolutionist hypothesis about the origin of religion which in turn has affected the disciplines of comparative religion and mythology too. Vedic culture or '*Āryadharma*' envisages a divinely given archetype which man needs to emulate and in the process fulfil as well as transcend his mere humanity or historic actuality. In such a view, man does start from a given empirical identity and does have to fulfil various obligations related to that, but the significance of this living and acting is determined by the earnestness with which he seeks his true transcendental identity. It is this seeking, this life-long process of self-realisation which came to be characterised as '*Sādhanā*'—the process of seeking and obtaining spiritual vision and inner transformation.

The true nature of man in the Vedic view is covered by a series of accidents or assumed personae. To each of these corresponds a way of viewing the world. The range of human experience extends from the inmost level of purely spiritual knowledge (in a Ramaṇa Maharṣi, for example) to the physical level of instinctive life. It follows therefore that appropriately lived life at each level is a preparation for transcending it. There is a beautiful metaphor used by *Ṛg Veda* to convey this urge: '*Yat sānoḥ sānumāruhat bhūri aspaṣṭa kartvam*' ('As he climbed from peak to peak, he espied evermore what was to be done').[7] 'A man is as big as his desire'—says D.H. Lawrence; but the question of all questions is: desire for what? Vedic literature gives an emphatic and unambiguous answer to this question when it declares that 'infinity alone can satisfy man' ('*Bhūmā vai sukham nālpe sukhamasti*'—Ch.U.7). In our own century, Sri Aurobindo, under Dayānanda's inspiration heroically took the Yogi's difficult way of personally grappling with the divine word of the Veda single-handed in a form of *Sādhanā* of which the *Ṛg Veda* is itself the unparalleled repository and teacher. Working his way, step by step in

7. Cited in '*The Secret of the Vedas*', Sri Aurobindo.

interpretation, he came to the conclusion that for getting at the living root of Hindu religiousness we have to go further back than the Upaniṣads, to the *Ṛg Veda* Samhitā itself. Being a poet himself, and dedicated since childhood to the service of the goddess Vāc he went back to the Veda, that very source where, in man's history for the first time this Divinity had revealed herself as a primordial and an omnipresent, pervasive power (*'yāvad Brahma viṣṭhitam tāvatī vāk'*—R.V., X.114.8d)—who makes of those upon whom she looks with favour into men of power, masters of the holy word, *ṛsis* and sages (*Yam kāmaye tantamugram kṛṇomi tam Brahmānam tamṛṣim tam sumedhām'*—R.V.X.125.5). Aurobindo's devotion to this goddess was abiding and his service to poetry as part of his *sādhanā* claimed him always though one wonders whether she commanded absolute and undivided loyalty from him. The Muse is said to be a jealous goddess and this testimony on the part of the western poet is rather difficult to dismiss although Indian experience by and large would appear to contradict it. In fact, some of the greatest poets in India have been saints or men of undoubted spiritual attainments. Even philosophers have composed poems: the incompatibility of the two vocations seems hardly to have bothered or even occurred to them. On the whole, it is the poet rather than the philosophic system-builder that seems to have performed the central role in determining and shaping Indian civilisation through the millennia. And this in itself is a glowing testimony to the subterranean presence of the ancestral voices that continued to be heard across the yawning gulfs and the inevitable ruptures in our historical existence.

Vedic *Sādhanā* does not presuppose any fixed theoretic or dogmatic system of thought but rather progressively discovers and reinterprets its presuppositions in the light of spiritual and cultural experiences. In this it is akin to art which does presuppose a felt and imaginative experience of the world which is quite distinct from any rational or pragmatic point of view. *Sādhanā* literally means making and that's also the meaning of 'poiesis'. 'It is myself that I remake'—says the poet Yeats in defence of his irresistible urge to rewrite his songs. To make a poem is, thus, at the deepest level of our being, a matter of making or remaking oneself. Now, it is a well-attested fact of Yogic experience and tradition that human nature can be transformed and raised above the shackles of greed, hatred and fear. That is an assumption built into the very texture of spiritual culture, which is essentially an insight into imponderable truth and value which subsists basically as personal communication but is expressed and elaborated through symbolic and intellectual activity. For instance, Uddālaka's communication '*tattvamasi*' to *Śvetaketu* in *Chāndogya Upaniṣad* gets elaborated in the schools of Advaitic philosophy on the one hand, and in the poetry of *Yogavāsiṣṭha* on the other. Coming to modern times, we see even Ramaṇa Maharṣi composing occasional devotional verses and even a great mystical genius like Rāmakṛṣṇa Paramhaṃsa availing himself frequently of the poetry which he found indispensable for the edification of his audience. Then there is the example of Aurobindo who saw no reason why poetry should not be a part of his *sādhanā*. But the question that we still find perplexing is: how exactly is yoga, that realm of silent wordless inward action related to the same man's unrelenting passion for the order of words? Here one finds oneself involuntarily recalling those words of Madam Blavatsky to young Yeats: 'Neither Buddha, nor Socrates ever wrote a book; for to do so would be reducing life to a logical process.' Wise words indeed! But both the great men were not averse to using words as such. And the Veda too was spoken word: now a text no doubt, but no book in the Jewish-Christian-Islamic sense. One is, nevertheless, perplexed by the polarity that does manifest itself between the prophet's way and the mystic's way—between one's direct access to the source of a clear and specific message and the other's realisation of a basically incommunicable experience. Does the over-arching category of '*Yoga*' encompass both and more?—one is left wondering. All one can safely affirm is that the way of the '*Muni*' is marked by the interiorization or actualization within the inner space of what is disclosed through the poetic operation with words in the 'Way of the *Ṛsi*'. Within the Indian tradition, its central Vedic experience as it has come to us through all its articulations and growth in time, seems to affirm the primacy of the word beginning with the role assigned to speech in the famous *Vāk-Ambhriṇi Sūkta*, but pervasive through the entire *Ṛg Veda Samhitā*. *Vāc* according to this hymn is not only the first of the whole Vedic pantheon, but, also the most unique because she is the mother attentive to the needs of both gods and men. She is "the thousand-syllabled speech dwelling in the highest regions of Transcendence, from where its inexhaustible plenty flows down to sustain everything that exists." Yet another verse, closely following this, tells us that, "of the four quarters into which speech is measured out, three are held in concealment, with only the fourth available for mortal use {R. V.1.164, 45)."

One became a seer not through hereditary office but only through actually attaining to the vision of the mantras. The word 'mantra' means that which has been thought or known and which possesses power to liberate. It is sacred speech, sacrificial formula, efficient councel. *Bṛhadāraṇyaka Upaniṣad* explains how the world came into being by the union of mind (*manas*) with word (*Vāc*). In Vedic view, every word is supposed to link up with the source of all words. The ultimate character of the word as God or Brahman is a fundamental concept in Indian spirituality. The Veda constituted by the mantras is thus at once wisdom as well as word. In later terminology it could be described as 'seeing speech' (*Paśyantī Vāk*). Let us hear the very first mantra called 'the *Gāyatrī*'.

Om bhūr bhuvah swaha
tat savitur vareṇyam
bhargo devasya dhīmahi
dhiyo yo nah pracodayāt.

The first line invokes the three worlds—earth, the space between sky and earth and heaven. The mantra is addressed to the divine life-giver as supreme God symbolized in *savitṛ*, the sun. It is recited by every Hindu householder daily at sunrise and at sunset. The mantra derives its name from the metre in which it is written—a meter of twentyfour syllables.

Since light is the predominant symbol of the Vedas, the *Gāyatrī* enjoys a unique distinction among mantras because it is a complete symbol of light. Each line emphasizes one aspect of light: the glory of the Ultimate and his own intrinsic radiance is celebrated in the first line, the world-illuminating radiance of the uncreated sun that is Savitṛ, the living God is suggested in the second line and the impact of this divine radiance on our mind converting us into light is suggested in the third. Thus it is union with the source of light, an ātman-brahman identity that is sought to be granted through this mantra.

The early Vedic religion was centred in prayer, inspiration and vision and envisaged the ideal of a full and happy human life virtuously and piously. Virtue and piety—far from being just passive principles are actively conceived. There is a perpetual struggle of right and wrong, light and darkness in which man must fight and serve and pray so that he may attain to the vision of light and participate on earth in the heroic victory of the gods. That is why the most famous of Vedic prayers which has continued to be offered right up to this day is a prayer for light as we have just now observed.

III

It is from a simple state of society and its natural setting that the hymns draw their symbols and images. Thus sunbeams at dawn are represented as herds of cows rushing out of the stall. Dawn itself is a lovely maiden waking up men and beasts. The sun is the eye of the gods or a glorious chariot racing across the sky. The Vedic poet responds to the daily miracle thus:

His mighty steeds advance
inexorably like a spider's web
rending the night's dark robe
How strange the sun! Untethered
unsupported he hangs in space
Why does he never fall?

This is from a *sūkta* in the fourth mandala of *Ṛg Veda*. In a hymn addressed to Varuṇa in the first mandala, the poet says,

Accompanying the Sombre Night
The stars like thieves now steal away
at the all-seeing sun's approach

Sūrya certainly means the sun. But the word comprehends a lot more than the sun. Savitṛ of the Gāyatrī mantra is also connected with the sun but is in no way identified with it. Other solar deities such as Bhaga, Āryaman, Pūṣan represent certain of the functions of the sun; but Sūrya comprehends the whole complex reality that the Vedic seer discovers in the sun. It is this constant preoccupation with light which appears to have given its name to the land itself. For Bhārat (that is India) literally means 'that which is obsessed with and dedicated to the pursuit of light.' The hymn to Sūrya presents him as 'pervading air and earth and heaven' and 'the soul of all that moves and moves not? This is how it concludes:

Gazing beyond the dark we reach
the supreme light and attain the sun
the God of gods, the light.

As Pūṣan the Sun-God is the protector of paths and pastures. As Savitṛ, he appears in a golden chariot in the twilight sky and sends men and beasts home. Apart from the sun, there is Indra, the Master of the universe, Agni, the friend of man, Varuṇa, the king of heaven and earth, Viṣṇu, the measurer of the three worlds and Soma, the hero. The most heroic aspect of Indra is liberation of the world from the domination of Vṛtra, the dragon producing drought and gloom. The dragon is slain by Indra with the help of Soma. The Maruts are a band of impetuous warriors riding through the billowing clouds and showering rain. The clouds are often imaged as mountain peaks and the atmosphere as a sea. Rudra is the archer par excellence and the poet entreats his arrows to avoid human habitations. Agni, the God of fire too occupies a prominent place in the Vedic pantheon. In fact, the *Ṛg Veda* opens with an invocation of Agni and concludes with dedication to him. He is the master of hearth and home, a loving father, a wise priest and, above all, a poet *par excellence.*' Varuṇa is a god-servant of Ṛta, that is, the cosmic order or law as well as Truth. In him all poetry centres like the hub in the wheel (R.V., Q.41.6). He enables truth to find expression in the formulation of the poet.

Then there is Dyāvā-Pṛthvī—heaven and earth—the primeval couple. In not a single hymn of *Ṛg Veda* is heaven mentioned alone. Celebrating this togetherness of Earth and Heaven, the poet sings:

> Which of these two came earlier, which came later
> How did they come to birth? Who, O seers can
> discern it?
> They contain within them all that has a name
> While days and nights revolve as on a wheel.

'The Hymn of Earth' is one of the most beautiful poems in the *Atharva Veda.* It is perhaps the longest one containing sixty three stanzas, and is enough by itself to prove that ecology was a sacred science for the Vedic Man.

> Whatever I dig up of you, O Earth,
> May you of that have a quick replenishment

> O purifying One, may my thrust never
> reach right into your vital points, your heart!

On the bosom of this earth, the streams are like laughing maidens, barley rejoices in the rain. Trees are majestic. The whole cycle of seasons as well as sunrise and sunset are celebrated. As for Parjanya, the rain-god, what an image to invoke and praise him!

> Like a bellowing bull with quickening streams
> He deposits a seed of life in the plants.

Then there is Araṇyāni—which literally means 'Wife of the Forest'—who is hailed with praises by the wind and the grasshopper. The unbounded expanse of nature is symbolized by Aditi. Sacrifice symbolises the process of creative transformation in nature, where gods are the sacrifices, Fire being the high priest. Rain from heaven is ritually imaged in the filtering of the soma juice through a woollen filter. The succession of Night and Day, the cycle of seasons, the sun and the moon and the stars in the heavens are all governed by the regulative power of *Ṛta*, which is the most fundamental Vedic concept. The concept arises from the basic Vedic *sādhanā* and experience of the holy word or prayer. The Brahman or prayer wells up from the heart and carries with it a revelation of the immutable power and self-governing nature of the gods. The power of Brahman and the power of the gods are bound up together as aspects of the same reality. It is *Ṛta* that is reflected in the cosmic order and it is *Ṛta* that governs the will of the gods who are, therefore called *Ṛtavrata*. *Ṛta* was never deified, because for the Vedic seers *Ṛta* was the ultimate source and origin of all beings including the gods.

Thus, the text of the Vedas in general and of the *Ṛg Veda* in particular discloses to us a world, which in the words of Prof. J.L. Mehta, philosopher and vedologist, is "the unifying play of the fourfold of earth and heaven, gods and mortals, in which man dwells on earth as his home, under the heavens, in friendly commerce with the gods, with his fellowmen and with things, building and making untiringly with thoughts and words and things."[8] Man here is always the mortal (*martyah*), desirous of earthly goods, needing help in the conduct of his life, unable to see clearly through the perils of existence, but aware of himself as a thinking being and of a light within as well as beyond him. He stands on this earth but is open to the heaven and responsive to the gods above who are themselves keen to respond to his call, and to kindle a light in the darkness within and without him. Man, if he is Ārya (i.e. hospitable to the guest from beyond, open to transcendence) and Brāhmaṇa dedicated to his creative vocation of wording the world, has but one all-consuming passion, the unceasing pursuit of light. It is not the infinite space of such a world that fills Vedic man with terror. If there is anything that terrifies him, it is *abhvam*, the black abyss of darkness and *ambas*, the sense of being constricted, the anguish of space closing in. To quote Prof. Mehta once again, "Light is the keyword of the great code that is this text, the central concept that illumines the text and holds it together as a unity, which unlocks its tropes, its symbolism and its mythic content."[9] The commonest word for man's ability to respond to light and inspiration is '*dhī*', but the variety of terms for what the mind of man is capable of, is as numerous as the words, symbols and metaphors for light. As we have already observed, the concern of Vedic poetry is practical, namely the actualization in one's own person of what it means to be fully human. This meaning according to Prof. Mehta, is brought out by the Vedic word '*varivas*', which recent research has redeemed from oblivion. The word means openness, to create an open space or clearing, to break through the cribbed and confined space of mortal life. The desire for this openness and for release from constriction, the creation of liberating space is conveyed by the word '*varivasyā*'.[10] The gods who appear to symbolise the consciousness of immortality for the mortal man are, therefore,

8. *Philosophy & Religion*, p. 278.
9. Ibid., p. 280.
10. *Kavikarma Aur Chintana*, J.L. Mehta.

'Varivaskṛta' or 'Varivodhā'. Indra and other Vedic gods each of whom is designated as poet, are supposed to perform precisely this function—to liberate the mortally 'conditioned' man from his confinement and help him to realise his freedom. Thus Agni is the burning flame of longing for self-transcendence. He is a thing among earthly things and also a symbol for the transactions between the human and the divine. As for the myth of the dragon *Vṛtra*, which literally names the force that covers and hides, blocks and thwarts, and of Indra slaying him and piercing and opening for the waters, the meaning is obviously connected with the word *Varivasyā*. Another myth with a metaphor at its core is that of the demon Vala, the encloser, the cavity that shuts in. Then there is the allied myth of the Pani demons who have hidden the cattle-treasure in the mountains. The central image in all these myths is that of light encapsulated within a rock, which Indra liberates with his power of shattering the impenetrable, with the thunderbolt, which in turn is often a symbol for poetic speech. Thus, within the text of *Ṛg Veda* iself, one may observe interpretive operations on the symbols going on, moving from one level of meaning to another, beginning with the processes of nature such as cloud-formation and rainfall, and culminating in the disclosure of light from a covering darkness. Clearly, this happens through the god-given brahman or poetic work, of the seers, in which each level of interpretation provides a symbol for the next higher.

IV

At this juncture, I find myself remembering an early letter of Tagore in which he records an experience of communion with nature which is simultaneously also the experience of communication with the mysterious power of consciousness:

> "My whole being melted and was fused with the earth. Yes, I had become the earth. I felt the green grass growing

over me, autumnal sunlight playing all over me and every pore of my verdant and moist body exuding the fragrant vapour of youth. I lay beneath the bright sky carrying the waters, plains and mountains of all the far and near lands in my arms. The autumn sun sent waves of bliss through me. This morning all that came alive to me—I felt the same emotion surging through me. I was the primeval earth itself—the sprouting, flowering, sun-bathed earth. It's as if the living stream of this very consciousness of mine is flowing through every blade of grass that grows on earth—every root and every branch of every tree on it...Oh, how I wish to express this...but everytime I am prevented by the disturbing thought of others. Others may not understand this feeling...others may not enter into this experience..."[11]

One can see that the experience described in this passage is near-mystical, advaitic in Upaniṣadic terms. But a shadow falls between the experience and the urge to express it—the shadow of the other. It disturb, naturally, because 'the other' ceases to exist as the other in the true Advaitic experience which is the experience of the one without the other.

Let us forget about mysticism and advaita. Let's respond to this account without thinking of mysticism or of upaniṣadic advaita. Let us respond to it as we respond to poetry pure and simple or to a poet's intimate journal. What do we feel? Doesn't this account correspond to the Vedic unitive vision of 'Hymn to the Earth' or '*Dyāvā-pṛthvī*'? Heaven and Earth as the original divine pair also appear to antedate the later proliferation of gods which was the result of treating the different aspects, names and attributes of '*Ekam Sat*', as different gods. The sense of the unity of Godhead is not just an intellectual conception. As an intellectual conception, it was doubtless formulated in later Vedic times, but this does not amount to saying that the religious feeling and mythical

11. Cited in 'A Selection from Tagore's Writings', pub. By Sahitya Akadami, New Delhi, in Hindi.

language of the earlier epoch had not been aware of the truth which was formulated later.

In fact modern materialism has distorted our response to matter itself. "How different was the former image of matter as the Great Mother"—says Carl Jung—"that could encompass and express the profound emotional meaning of Mother Earth!" "Similarly", he goes on to say, "what was the spirit is now identified with intellect and thus ceases to be the father of all. It has degenerated to the limited ego-thoughts of man; the immense emotional energy expressed in the image of our Father vanishes into the sand of an intellectual desert."[12]

What prevented the Upaniṣadic Adhyātma-yoga from leading to nihilism was the identification of the Ātman with the Brahman, where Brahman was the creative cosmic principle. The eternal spiritual principle is at once the ground of subjective as well as of objective being. Quest for the ground of one's own empirical being and quest for the ground of the world without meet at the same point. That is the final spiritual experience which the Upaniṣads give expression to. As the Āraṇyakas developed the notion of sacrifice into that of *upāsana* or symbolic meditation, the Upaniṣads went beyond *upāsanā* to the pure path of enquiry or Jñāna yoga. The Upaniṣadic sensibility cannot and ought not to be distinguished too sharply from the Vedic sensibility. Both are Vedic tradition. The Upaniṣadic quest for Brahman was not a purely intellectual quest (as in Greek culture). The truth it sought was not a value-neutral truth. *Brahmavidyā* or metaphysics was interpreted as *Ātma-vidyā* i.e., self-knowledge or spiritual science. Although dialectical in the original Socratic sense, its method was frequently intuitive and analogical rather than purely logical or conceptual. Its mode of enquiry is certainly not aimed at the conceptual control of the universe as the western mode by and large does seem to have become. It sought a spiritual truth and it sought to achieve the experience of it. Naturally therefore, the literary means adopted for communicating this

12. Carl Jung, *Approaching the Unconscious: Man and his Symbols.*

experience are dialogue, parable and poetry rather than strict ratiocination. That is what makes the Upaniṣadic sense and sensibility continuous with and part of the Vedic tradition as a whole. Blending poetry and prose, the mystical and the philosophical, the Upaniṣads are the inheritors of an early search for cosmological truth as well as for the 'mystery' which would lead to personal immortality. What makes the Upaniṣadic thought unique is the identification of Brahman with Ātman. Philosophically the Upaniṣads combine the cosmological enquiry for the first cause with the psychological enquiry for the self. That the two quests, for the ground of one's own empirical and psychic being within and for the ground of the world without meet at the same point is the final spiritual experience which the Upaniṣads give expression to. Speculative reasoning may have helped in this, but the principle of advaita really rests on spiritual testimony. It is only when the mind is turned away from objects and is still and one-pointed that it becomes illuminated by the intuitive realization of the self. The decisive plunge into realization requires the grace of the Self, for the identity of Ātman and Brahman implies that the Self is the divine reality.

Some of the Upaniṣads do stress the divinity of the Self. In the *Īṣopaniṣad* and at times in *Kaṭhopaniṣad*, the Self is a personal god who pervades the whole universe and is at the same time, the spirit in man. To know the Self then is to know one's identity with all. At some other places, most significantly in *Śvetāśvatara* Upaniṣad, God is distinguished from the individual soul. Here we have a clear adumbration of Yoga as well as Bhakti which is mentioned by name in this Upaniṣad for the first time. Let me quote a few lines from this Upaniṣad to suggest the continuity as well as the subsequent evolution of the sacred poetry we have been talking about so far:

> Thou art the fire
> Thou art the sun
> Thou art the moon

Thou art the starry firmament,
Thou art Brahman supreme:
Thou art the waters-thou
The creator of all!
Thou art woman, thou art man
Thou art the youth, thou art the maiden
Thou art the old man tottering with his staff
Thou facest every where.

Thou art the dark butterfly
Thou art the green parrot with red eyes,
Thou art the thundercloud, the seasons, the seas.
Without beginning art thou
Beyond time, beyond space
Thou art he from whom sprang
the three worlds.
... ...

Thou Brahman Immortal,
and thou, woven of clay
(Two beings, yet one)-
Like two beautiful birds,
Golden of plumage,
Companions inseparable
Perched high up on the branches
Of the self-same tree-
As man thou tastest-
The sweet fruits of the tree,
The sweet and bitter fruit
But as Brahman, master of Maya
Thou remainst unseen, immobile
Calmly observing.
Forgetting his oneness with thee
Bewildered by his weakness,
Full of sorrow is man;
But let him look close on thee,

know thee as himself
O Lord, most worshipful
And behold thy glory-
Lo, all his heavy sorrow-
Is turned to joy.

Changeless thou art,
Supreme, pure!
In thee dwell the gods.
The source of all scriptures thou art;
Yet what shall scriptures avail
If they be smooth on the lip
But absent from the heart?
To him who knows thee comes fullness-
To him alone!... ... ..."[13]

V

It's time for me to stop here. But before I do so, I would like to gather together again, some thoughts and images scattered in the *Ṛg Veda* which you have already come across in the course of this rather sprawling, but I hope, not very incoherent lecture.

> Let the threads that bind us to divinity not be broken. Let the sacred threads by which we weave the coloured web of our song remain intact. May we not lose track of the paths that run between the gods and men, not fail in our contractual hospitality to the immortal that has come as a guest in the mortal's house. May we not lost sight of the trace left behind by the bird of flight.[14]

13. *The Upaniṣads,* Swami Prabhavananda and Frederick Manchester, pp. 123-127.
14. Cited by J.L. Mehta, 'The Hindu Tradition', in *Philosophy & Religion*, p. 107.

That, in a nutshell, ladies and gentlemen, was the single all-overriding concern of the Vedic *ṛṣis*, as indeed in all the subsequent phases of Indian religious life. For the Vedic poet, as for ourselves, there are ever-present possibilities of the oppressive closure of sacred space. We saw how he made use of the particularities of his ambience, like all poets, to hammer out a language and a ritual of making sacred (sacrifice), and to present a vision that ensures inalienable closeness to the sacred for mankind. You will have noticed, I hope, that although the particularities of historical chance are, in this literature, never dwelt on, there nevertheless was a history: a community of shared vision on the march, with memory of a beginning, awareness of present crisis and a voice that spoke into the future. In my subsequent lectures, I propose to look into that history and that future. Meanwhile my memory has conjured up this prayer of a 20th century Spanish poet, which I offer to you as a befitting conclusion to this lecture.

> Intelligence, give me
> The exact name of things
> Let my word be the thing itself
> Newly created by my soul
> Through me may all those
> Who have forgotten things reach them
> Through me may all those
> Who even love things may reach them.

–Juan Ramon Jimenez

Ancestral Voices in the Post-Vedic

From Mirror after mirror
No vanity's displaced
I'm looking for the face I had
Before the world was made[1]

—W.B. Yeats

and the Classical Ages of Sanskrit Poetry

I

Ancient Sanskrit literature, like the Vedic epiphany it succeeded belongs not just to India, but to the heritage of mankind. Or, we might better put it this way: it belongs to the heritage of mankind precisely because it is the creation of men who were dedicated from the dawn of human history itself to the articulation and realisation of that destiny of humankind which, as we saw with Carl Jung yesterday, was and is the quest for light, that is, the creation of more and more consciousness. Not only the ancient mind; but even the agnostic-secular modern mind at its acutest and deepest has been compelled to look beyond its own premises to retrieve the irretrievable in its anguished obsession with the fact of consciousness itself. "What is the nature of the inalterability of the mind through all its own activity, the action of the universe upon it, the slow decay of the organism to which it is attached?"—asks Paul Valery in one of his seminal essays. "The answer"—he says, "is consciousness, in its most abstract form." Valery makes a distinction between consciousness and personality. "Personality", he say, is "only a thing mutable and accidental beside this most naked self."

Now, isn't it a fact, ladies and gentlemen, if only once you come to think of it, that the greatest minds define themselves, not in terms of the personality but in terms of this Self which has no name and no history, which is no more perceptible and no less real than the centre of gravity of a ring or a planetary system? Well, this is for the poet Valery the goal to be attained,

---

1. W.B. Yeats, 'A Woman Young and Old' in C.P., p. 308.

where the mind feels itself to be pure consciousness—where there really can't be two. Now, a truly precise one-pointed mind can understand itself in certain states. That's why it is unknowable. There are no names for the things among which one is really alone. It is the face without the mirror, a mirror where one looks at oneself and which gives one the desire to talk to oneself.

But, 'looking for the face one had before the world was made', as the poet has put it, may take the modern mind and sensibility in a different direction than the one taken by Valery. One immediately thinks of a poet like Holderlin who had his own way of coming to terms with the fact of what he so poignantly sought to articulate as 'the departure of the gods'. Yesterday we were talking about Vedic poetry and today we propose to talk about its successor—the ancient Sanskrit poetry. But why? Why should we bother about things which are so remote from us in time and space if something in our own immediate situation doesn't call for it? And here no one's testimony is more reliable and more revealing than that of a poet, so far as a true picture and definition of that immediate situation itself is in question. Poets like Yeats, Valery and Holderlin, for example do enable us to look into the heart of darkness. "And what are poets for in a destitute time?"—asks Holderlin's elegy 'bread and wine'. "His answer, as interpreted by Heidegger is that, "the gods who were once here, return only at the right time—that is, when there has been a turn among men in the right place, in the right way."[2] That's what Holderlin's unfinished hymn 'Mnemosyne' also seems to suggest:

> ...The heavenly powers
> Cannot do all things. It is the mortals
> Who reach sooner into the abyss. So the turn is
> With these. Long is the time
> But the true comes into its own.

---

2. Heidegger, *Poetry, Language, Thought*, p. 92.

And what about ourselves—our own pre-theoretical consciousness of every day life—our particular social life-world? For us too, it would seem, the task of new linguistic formulation remains all important: as poets or intellectuals we just can't afford to relinquish responsibility taking refuge in 'cultural continuities' or 'the modernity of tradition' etc. As one of our own contemporary philosophers puts it, "the only way in which the potency and seminal power of the primal words of our own sacred tradition can become meaningful to us again is a creative linguistic construction—a more active conversation with our sacred texts."[3] After all, it is the conversational apparatus that is supposed to maintain what counts as reality in a society at any particular time. It is necessary, therefore, to remember at the very outset the general difference between ancient and modern literatures. Modern literature is agnostic and secular and its social awareness is historical. It is also individualistic in the sense that it regards the expression of the individual psyche in its particularity as a value. If an ancient poet—Vyāsa or Vālmīki, for example—were to look at modern poetry, he would be surprised at our obsession with the particular and the ephemeral. On the other hand, ancient literature would appear to us equally remote with our modern taste for subjectivity, democracy, naturalism and stream of consciousness etc. It is necessary to take cognisance of this because, as one of our great scholars has pointed out, several modern writers on Sanskrit have tended to disparage it in terms drawn from the critique of classicism by the Romantics. But Sanskrit literature is neither classical like Greeko-Roman literature nor classicist like 17th and 18th century English or French literatures. At the same time, we must not think of it entitled only to the opinions of its own ancient critics according to traditional standards.

Whether it be ancient or modern, we value literature for the insight it gives us into values and for the imaginative experience which moves us at a different and a deeper level

3. Prof. J.L. Mehta, *Philosophy and Religion*, p. 253.

than actual life does. It's a value, an experience which cuts across the historical distinctions of Romanticism and classicism and according to our ancient tradition, this imponderable and felt experience of value, which it chooses to designate as 'Rasa', constitutes the 'real' meaning of a literary work. All other meanings and words are only the medium for the revelation of '*rasa*'. As Prof. G.C. Pande—a profound Sanskrit scholar as well as renowned historian has pointed out, "Rasa, mistranslated sentiment, is manifested in terms of experience but is really a quality belonging to the spirit. The intuition of '*rasa*', infact, is nothing except a self-realisation in terms of imaginative experience('*bhāvāvachbhinna-cidāvaraṇa-bhanga*', which literally means "a rending of the veil that conceals reality that is consciousness from us imprisoned and constricted beings").[4] "Since it is an empirical self-realisation in imagination, '*rasa*' may present itself as the essence of the most diverse characters, situations and responses. This is not the place to undertake a detailed consideration of the theory of Rasa. We've reserved that for our next lecture. Suffice it to say here that it's the philosophical concept of '*rasa*' with which we are concerned here and not with the classification of rasas as such, with which the general theory of '*rasa*' is usually connected. At first, only eight rasas were recognised. Then a ninth *Śānta rasa* (the aesthetic state of perfect quiescence or repose) was added mainly because of the epic *Mahābhārata*. Ānandavardhana, the great aesthetician held that the dominant rasa of that epic was *Śānta rasa*. It was only in the 16th century that *bhakti* came to be recognised as a *rasa* in itself. The classification that recognises *Vīra* (heroic), *Śṛngāra* (romantic-erotic) and *Śānta* (quiescence) as the three principal rasas is not always quite adequate and foolproof to describe either Vedic poetry or the epics or the subsequent classical Sanskrit literature. As we have already observed, the earliest phase of Vedic poetry or Upaniṣadic prose and verse is characterized by the heroic spirit of man, by his sense of wonder, delight or

4. G.C. Pande, *Foundations of Indian Culture*, p. 274.

peace based on spiritual enlightenment. *Vīra rasa*, however is quite inadequate to characterize the sublimity of such a cosmic or spiritual vision. In the early post-vedic phase, one can behold the tradition of *Śānta rasa* emerging in the ascetic poetry of the Brāhminical, Buddhist or Jain varieties. This poetry is distinguishable by a sense of world-sorrow, resignation and quiescence rather than by that of life-affirming joy and harmony characteristic of the Vedic age. Alongside this, we have the heroic poetry of the two epics. In the classical age, the heroic idea persists but is diluted with the gradual decline of the aristocracy. The other major theme of classical poetry is love and here also erotic sensuousness gradually came to predominate in *Śṛngāra*. Kālidasa and Bhavabhūti belonging to the earlier phase of the classical age treat of heroism and romance (That is, *Vīra* and *Śṛngāra*) within a wholesome and balanced view of life. After the 8th century A.D., however, there appears rigidity and imbalance in society and religion leading to self-indulgence and lack of sense of proportion in poetry too. The poetry of Śriharṣa may be said to mark the culmination of this period.

"Never was poetry held in higher esteem and its nature and purpose conceived more exaltedly than in the early Vedic age", says Sri Aurobindo. Poetry, vision and wisdom were held to be identical. The human poet was a counterpart of the Divine because the Vedic seers felt that vision, form and rhythm really belong to the Divine mind. Nothing exemplifies this better than the testimony of *Īśāvāsyopaniṣad* itself, where God is called "Poet, Seer, Creator and Fashioner of Forms."[5] In fact, the Upaniṣadic concept of Saccidānanda Brahma has its origin and authentication in the poetry of the *Ṛg Veda*. The vision of this poetry is that of the inherent value and sublimity of Being. Delight of existence is the very basis of it. The cosmos is the manifestation of a divine order and this order called *Ṛta,* is manifested in the working of divine forces. Thus the hymns

5. 'Kavirmanīṣī paribhūh Swayambhū Yāthārthyatorthān Vyadadhācchāśvatibhyah Samābhyah.'

to Agni are hymns not only to the presiding spirit of the home and the hearth but also to the spirit of prayer and poetry. In fact, the preoccupation with the Word (*Vāc*) and the creative process there is, as we saw yesterday, one of the basic concerns of the Vedic poet. Yet another important concern of the Vedic seers, which couldn't be touched upon yesterday, is the idea of governance, the wielding of wise and virtuous authority. Indra, Varuṇa and Mitra constitute the symbols of such authority. Kālidāsa, the greatest poet of the classical age in his epic poem '*Raghuvaṃśa*' presents us in the figure of Raghu with an image of the ideal king which reminds us of those Vedic symbols. In fact some of the dominant metaphors and myths used in the Ṛg Veda and other Vedas can be seen to reappear throughout the subsequent developments of Indian poetry and most significantly in the works of Kālidāsa himself, as we hope to demonstrate as briefly as possible towards the end of this lecture.

But we were talking about the Vedic God Indra. We have already looked at the hymns in his praise which speak of war and conflict, power and victory, valour and exhilaration. The hymns of Varuṇa and Mitra celebrate the majesty of cosmic law and sovereignty. Both have their own appropriate imagery. If lightning and thunder symbolise the striking power of Indra, the star-studded night-sky (*Sfuṭacandratārakā*' as Kālidāsa in his epic '*Kumāra Sambhava*' rephrases the image) symbolizes the eternal vigilance of cosmic law. The Maruts correspond to the common people just as Agni and Indra correspond to Brahman and Kṣatra that is, to the priestly intellectual class on the one hand and the man of action on the other. The archetypal persistence of this symbolism can be perceived in all subsequent literature. No poetic discourse can be completely demythologised. But if we try to grasp the essential import of the epic Mahābhārata, it can be put simply thus: that *brahma* and *kṣatra*, together and intermixed are essential to human living; that *kṣatra* divorced from *brahma* is self-destructive; that *Brahma* subservient to *kṣatra* can only spell disaster; that *kṣatra* serving *Brahma* ensures excellence in war and peace; that the two in concord and under the guidance of *Kṛṣna* (Supreme Spirit, God) constitute the perfection within reach of man. The same principle is applicable according to *Mahābhārata* to the three ends of human endeavour (*Puruṣārthas*) also. They too give fulfilment to man only when they are held together in balance and steered by guidance from *kṛṣna* (that is, God as friend). Apart from the *Bhagavadgītā*, which forms part of the epic, the central insight into the meaning of war and peace is, according to Prof. J.L. Mehta, perhaps provided by *Kṛṣna* in his exhortation to Yudhiṣṭhira, seeking to persuade him not to shirk his duty as a king. It is noteworthy how Kṛṣna invokes the central myth from the *Ṛg Veda* to persuade Yudhiṣṭhira. Here are the words of Kṛṣna to Yudhiṣṭhira (translated into English by Prof. Mehta):

> "All devious thinking and acting bears the mark of death; rectitude alone is the place of Brahma. You have not yet completed the conquest of your enemies, for the chief and sole enemy is within you. Even Indra was able to destroy Vṛtra only by seeking him out within himself. Remember the hurts of the past. A combat of the same magnitude as your fight with Bhīṣma and Droṇa is facing you, a combat without weapons, not with another, but with your own mind, with your own self. '*Mama*' (mine) is the two lettered death, 'na mama' (not mine) is the three-lettered eternal brahma, both of which are within us, impelling us to fight (*Āśvamedhika Parva*, ch.13)."[6]

Here, we have to remind ourselves that 'na mama' is part of the central formula in all sacrificial offering.

6. Mahābhārata—Āśvamedhika Parva, ch.13 quoted by Prof. J.L. Mehta in his essay on 'The Discourse of violence in the Mahābhārata'.

II

The **Rāmāyana** and the **Mahābhārata** quite unlike ***Iliad*** or *Aeneid* are gargantuan epics. The word *itihāsa*, perhaps better fits literary phenomena like the twin Indian epics. According to Sri Aurobindo, 'an *itihāsa* was an ancient historical or legendary tradition turned to creative use as a significant myth or tale expressive of some spiritual or religious meaning, and thus formative of the mind of the people.'[7] There is no doubt that these twin epics have played the biggest role in shaping the mind and attitudes of the Indian people. Tradition has invested Vālmīki with the mantle of Ādi Kavi—the first poet, and it may cause some surprise keeping in view the great heritage of Vedic sacred poetry. Perhaps that's why Aurobindo says that "Vālmīki, the father of our secular poetry, stands for that early and finely moral civilisation which was the true heroic age of the Hindu spirit; while Vyāsa, who came later, stood still farther on into the era of aristocratic turbulence and disorder." Both epics belong to the tradition of heroic poetry but heroism in the Indian epics operates at two levels. At one level, the hero is a mighty warrior, at another the moral dimension of his character is too pervasive to be called secondary. The magnanimity of Rāma and the truthfulness of Yudhiṣthira for example, set them quite apart from all other epic heroes and yet they are felt to be profoundly human. Rāvana, Rāma's adversary in Vālmīki's epic is as brilliant a display of the poet's imaginative powers as Rāma himself. But one doesn't feel the kind of ambiguity one feels in the case of, say, Milton's creation of Satan. Both the epics distinguish the true heroic spirit from the false one and although no one who really reads these epics can complain of a lack of tragic sense in them, they do not constitute ultimate tragedies. Perhaps that's the reason why Tagore described the epics as 'eternal history'. They represent the basic patterns of human life as seen from the point of view of high moral idealism.

7. Sri Aurobindo, The Foundations of Indian Culture.

The characters of the *Mahābhārata* and *Rāmāyana* have been more real and vivid through the ages in Hindu imagination than any historical characters. Sri Aurbindo rightly ascribes more of 'thought in action' to *Mahābhārata* and more of 'thought in repose' to the *Rāmāyaṇa*. The former, according to him, pictures a time of gigantic ferment and disturbance, and the later an age of equipoise, order and tranquility. The *Rāmāyana* does certainly bear the stamp of a recognisable individual tone and style, but the *Mahābhārata* too is a unified creative work at once poetic and intellectual, *kāvya* and *smṛti* in one. Here the view of Śri Aurobindo seems much more illuminating and much more to the point than the views of western historians of Sanskrit literature like Winternitz and Hopkins. "The *Mahābhārata*" according to Aurobindo is "the creation and expression of a collective national mind. It is the poem of a people about themselves."

I have seen an illiterate woman from chhattisgarh enact the *Mahābhārata* in her own dialect and hold an urban sophisticated audience spellbound for hours. I've listened to a band of Muslim singers from Rājasthān sing the *Mahābhārata* in their own dialect and keep a similar urban audience enthralled in the same way. One wonders however, whether with this growing mania for state patronage, and with the rank politicisation of rural life as well, all is still well with the traditional character of the rural communities themselves which had the resourcefulness to ensure such vital continuities with their cultural heritage. That illiterate woman and those Muslim singers certainly had a much more intimate relationship with the ethos of the *Mahābhārata* than our university graduates and even teachers can boast of. But the disturbing question that occurs to one nevertheless, is: What about the future of such vibrant cultural continuities themselves: Are they not threatened with distortion and debasement through these very efforts to patronise and preserve them?

A thorough study of the epic as *kāvya*, (as poetry) still remains a challenging task for the future. Only such a deep engagement with it can reveal how the various aspects of the poem—the mythic and the sacred, the human and the moral, the narrative and the didactic meet and coalesce to form a coherent whole; how the epic poem comprehends and makes use of the already ancient Vedic tradition to illumine its altered present and how it looks forward to the future towards which it reaches out, how the temporal conditioning of man is here brought into relation with the eternality of the divine. For, this is not an '*itihāsa*' in the sense in which, according to Aristotle, history is opposed to poetry. It is poetry comprehending the past, but reaching out to the future. It talks of the past, as all narrative must, only to be able to say something truly, comprehensively cosmic. This is apparent from the design, from the way it is said at the beginning and again towards the end of the epic that, of the pupils to whom kṛṣna Dwaipāyana *Vyāsa*, the author, narrated this tale, Nārada recited it to the Gods, Asita Devala to the Ancestors, his son Śuka to the *gandharvas*, *yakṣas* and *rākṣasas*, and *Vaiśaṃpāyana* to the mortals. What message is thus sought to be transmitted to the far corner of this created universe, from what necessity, and under what urgent need?

It is the pre-eminence of Dharma in human living which is the central theme of the *Mahābhārata*. Rooted in the three worlds, its sacred geography and cosmology, as also the presence in it of beings who are somehow above the usual human state, provide the context in which this concern is exhibited; an inner freedom from the life of desire puts this in perspective. Beyond this, however, there is a vision here of *kṛṣna* as the ultimate, transcending principle, suggesting a total revaluation of the traditional conceptual framework. If I have chosen to dwell on this epic rather longer than on other literature so far, it is because this epic has been regarded as a sort of fifth Veda—comprehending the whole accumulated experience of a people. A study of the topography, the human and non-human ethnography and of the epiphanies and hierophanies in it will demonstrate how the structuring of space in it is related to time, to man's captivity in it or to his ability to transcend it. This will reveal the vital links the world of the

Mahābhārata still maintains with the more ancient world of the Vedic ancestors. Often the collapse of time and space is marked by the appearance of message-bearers and other divine, semi-divine and even demonic beings who turn up at critical junctures to influence the course of events. Kṛṣna himself is the foremost of these but there are other gods as well. Over and above it all, it's the figure and role of another Kṛṣna—Kṛṣna Dwaipāyana *Vyāsa*, the author of this epic, which deserves close attention.

He is not only the creator of this epic but also the begetter of the three brothers—the Sage Vidura as well as Dhṛtarāṣtra and Pāndū—the fathers of the warring Kauravas and Pāndavas. That his mother is a low-caste fisher girl is connected with the fact that this fifth Veda is intended to reach all those who are not able to receive the revelatory secret wisdom of the original Vedas. Far from disappearing behind his work, Vyāsa enters on several occasions into the story itself. This island-like (Dvaipāyana), unattached but compassionate author feels obliged to console, pacify and advise the characters created by himself. It is as if he felt personally responsible for them in some way and needed to tell them that they are not just the playthings of his creative propensity; that inspite of all their pangs and misfortunes, all manner of things shall be well in the end. Prof. Mehta in his most sensitive and insightful reading of this epic[8] has laid particular emphasis on a special knowledge called '*pratismṛti*' which is a '*brāhmaṇa*' or sacred word analogous to the vedic mantra which had the potency of making things manifest and disclose their real nature. He tells us that according to Sāyaṇa, the 14th century commentator on *Ṛg Veda*, '*pratismṛti*' is a request to the gods to approach. And in the epic, as in the original *Ṛg Veda* as well, it is indeed Indra who comes to Arjuna in response to Arjuna's invocation of him through the *brāhmaṇa* or mantra that he has learnt from Vyāsa. Thus Vyāsa is a *ṛṣi*, a descendent of Vedic Vaśiṣṭha, a title lower than the gods but above ordinary mortals. We are

8. J.L. Mehta, 'Krishna Dvaipāyana: Poet of Being and Becoming', in Philosophy & Religion, p. 221.

left in no doubt that as author too, he is himself the supreme master of visionary experience, which he occasionally permits others to share.

The most poignant moment in the epic is the last scene where we see this author for the last time, when he is sitting alone, for once disconsolate because Kṛṣna himself has departed. Arjuna, after he has had a terrifying experience of his utter impotence without the Divine friend, approaches him in despair and narrates the incidents of the self-destruction of Kṛṣna's clan, of Kṛṣna's death and of his own terrible humiliation. "From the moment I heard"—he says, "that Kṛṣna has departed, there is nothing but darkness around me. I've lost my bearings in this world and no longer wish to live. Tell me what I'm to do." Vyāsa tells him not to grieve for it was all destined to be so. Then, for the first time, we hear this Kṛṣna speaking about that other Kṛṣna.

> "He, the Lord of the three worlds, could have prevented the catastrophe, but chose not to. He was the ancient *Ṛṣi* Nārāyaṇa who gave you his companionship and guidance out of his love for you. But he is now gone as his work on earth at this time is completed. For you and your brothers too, the time has now come to depart. That is best for you."[9]

I would like to close this account of the *Mahābhārata* with the most insightful comment of Prof. J.L. Mehta on these words of *Vyāsa*.

> "Nara, man as a being who dares, is what he is through Nārāyana, the ground of his own being. Now that the story of the interplay between the two, of this two-in-one, has been told, the author too relinquishes his authorial function as a servant of the goddess of speech and reverts to his proper status as a muni, one who meditates in silence. By virtue of his creative imagination—shall we call it

9. Ibid., pp. 223-234.

'*pratismṛti*'—the power to see and give form to the truth of things—he gave shape to his narrative and to his characters, with only Kṛṣna as the reality transcending his authorial grasp, not at his disposal. Relating what happened in time, he aims at revealing what always is, that which constitutes the truth of man's way of being in the world."[10]

III

Vālmīki and Vyāsa were the last of the seer-poets. After them begins the 'classical' age of Sanskrit literature. The accent now falls differently: the main concern is now humanistic and aesthetic. The blessings and enjoyment of human life as such, the endless seeking of the joys of love and the fascination of beauty, of verbal patterns and rhythms now acquire an autonomous value. In no other poetry perhaps, has plastic imagination found such consummate expression. Kālidāsa, called *kavi-kula guru*, the teacher of all poets—occupies the centre-stage here. He does claim to follow in the footsteps of Vālmīki, but there are hardly signs of any actual borrowing of image or phrasing in his poetry from Vālmīki. That is why, the subterranean presence of some dominant metaphors from *Ṛg Veda* in his work assumes all the deeper significance. It has been claimed that no other poet walked upon the earth with such sensitiveness to the beauty of nature or of the feminine form and that no other poet had so vivid imagination. He is credited with not only the discovery of the genre of describing the cycle of seasons in *Ṛtusambāra*, but also with his '*Meghadūta*', of having been pioneer in the creation of *dutakāvyas*. He has been acknowledged as the master of *Vaidarbhī* style, where the perfect correspondence between word and meaning leads to a marvellous transparency. Like the union of Śiva and Śakti—the parents of this universe—this union of word and meaning creates an infinite world of *rasa*.

10. Ibid., p. 225.

That is exactly what he invokes at the very outset of his long poem '*Raghuvaṃśa*'.[11] His art lies in concealing art. As evidence of his expressive imagery, we may look at a much-quoted verse from the second act of Śākuntala. King Duṣyanta, who has a passion for hunting has, since his encounter with Śakuntalā, lost all interest in the strenuous pursuit. From being the hunter of beasts in the woodland, the king is transformed into what he really should have been, their protector. And this transformation is wrought by love. But all this is subtly suggested through the imagery. The nearby buffaloes, the deer further on, and boars still farther off are resting, each in its own way and the woodland is quiet. The hunter's bow is relaxed.

The cycle of seasons has been of perennial interest to Indian poets. Ṛtusamhāra opens with the oppressive heat of summer and ends with the joy of spring. The hot wind of summer "crackles with shrill shouting in the dry bamboo reaches": '*Sphuṭati paṭuninādah śuṣkavaṃśasthalīṣu*'. The rainclouds are looked upon as saviours of the suffering people ("*Santaptānām tvamasi śaraṇam*"). In '*Meghadūta*' the poet gives us a fantastic aerial survey of the ever-changing landscape of India. The second half of the poem (translated into English during the Romantic era by H.H. Wilson) soars beyond the heat and rain of the Indian plains with their rivers and towns, fields and hills to the lofty Himālayas beyond which lies the city of Alakāpurī 'ever-illumined by the moonlight streaming from the moon on Śiva's forehead'. In this heavenly city lies the home of the beloved of the forlorn demi-god (yakṣa). Presently he is banished to a place far away from his beloved. But he hopes that somehow destiny will take a turn for the better for him and reunite him with his beloved.

This sense of present loss owing to some past misdeed and the yearning and hope for future redemption through suffering and sacrifice is a recurrent theme in Kālidāsa. If

11. Vāgarthāviva Sampṛktau Vāgartha pratipattaye Jagatah pitarau vande parvat parmeśwarau

'*Meghadūta*' exhibits it in the personal domain, *Raghuvaṃśa*—which according to the British indologist A.B. Keath, is the maturest work of Kālidāsa—exhibits it in the public sphere. Tagore somewhere points out how the epic breathes the despondency of political decline but still hopes for a bright future. '*Kumārasaṃbhava*', its natural sequel, has a profound theme in mythical form. For the birth of Kumāra who would lead the divine host, Śiva and Śakti must come together and for that possibility to become actualized, Śakti—that is Pārvatī, daughter of the Himālayas must purify herself through austerities (*tapas*).

The theme of true love forged through suffering is taken up, again, on a human plane this time, in the famous Śākuntala. Duṣyanta's love for Śākuntala is aroused in the midst of chase in an earthly forest; but then it has to pass through the pangs of separation, amnesia and remorse till it is finally fulfilled in the heavenly hermitage beyond violence and evil.

Bhāravi and Māgha come next. Bhāravī's *Kirātārjunīyam* is characterised by poetic intelligence rather than imagination. Māgha's '*Śiśupālavadha*' has a distinct though subdued undertone of devotional adoration. Māgha's poetry dazzles us by learning and rhetoric rather than the rarer qualities of imagination. Śrīharṣa on the other hand has the rare distinction of being a great philosopher as well as a poet. He is sonorous rather than picturesque.

The last, but not the least among the dramatist poets is Bhavabhūti. Like Euripedes in Greek drama, he is distinguished by his delicate sensibility and a deep tragic sense. He himself declares that the only basic feeling which man could honestly entertain about life was that of sorrow and pity. His depiction of the love between Rāma and Sītā in '*Uttara Rāmacarita*' is remarkable for its tenderness and pathos. He evinces an unusual feeling for the cruel aspects of nature. He is deservedly proud of his verbal mastery as the opening verse of his celebrated play shows: '*Yam Brahmāṇamiyam Devī vāk vaśyevānuvartate*'. ('I am the poet whom the goddess of speech loves to follow'.)

IV

There are works which appear to be of foundational importance in the establishment and further evolution of a whole cultural tradition. But this evolution, this development is brought about not by imitation, but by rediscovery and re-interpretation in very much altered times. Subsequent poets discover entirely new meanings in the ancient works. They are enabled to do so only by responding fully to the tendencies and challenges of their own times. That's how Kṛṣna Dvaipāyan Vyāsa created *Mahābhārata* and that's how Kālidāsa came to inaugurate a new world of sensibility. Every work comes to be encrusted by the accumulated experiences and expressions of the race in time. But time also serves to remove these encrustations. Time, which creates distance serves also, paradoxically, to refine our vision and bring far distant works close to us. The flow of Time is a continuum: poetry itself is shaped by time. In a special sense, poetry can be called the luminous form of time itself.

Thinkers all the world over are more and more coming to recognise the fact that the dawn as well as the development of every major culture, its distinctive character and flavour rest upon certain primeval metaphors fundamental to it. These metaphors and the myths made out of them may lose their vitality in subsequent periods of time and others may come to replace them. Nevertheless their pressure and memory is somehow retained in the unconscious levels of that culture. In the new historic milieu and the new creativity, those seed-metaphors come to sprout and flower again.[12] How such seed-metaphors of the earliest beginnings of a culture can still retain their creative potential can be best illustrated from Kālidāsa. Kālidāsa begins his epic poem *Raghuvaṃśa* with a humble admission of his meagre talents. He wonders how in spite of

12. For the deep reading of these seed–metaphors, I am indebted to the late Prof. J.L. Mehta's lectures delivered in Hindi at the Vatsala Foundation, New Delhi, and now available in book-from, under the title 'Kavikarma aur Chintana'.

such self-knowledge he dares to aspire to poetic fame. Then in the next verse he conceives this metaphor to find some justification for such an aspiration: '*Athavā kṛt vāgdwāre vaṃśesmin pūrvasūribhih*': "The ancient poets have opened a door of speech where formerly no such possibility of getting entrance existed. It is as if they have pierced a hole through the impenetrable gem. All I have to do now is to get through the hole like a thread." The implication is that the first breakthrough was made by the first poet and the poet of a different time gave a new turn to poetry to enable it to word a new world and a new age. The overt reference is to Vālmīki of course, whom tradition honours as the *ādikavi*—the First Poet. But we know that the Ganges of Indian poetry has its source in a much more ancient time than the age of Vālmīki The verse just quoted uses two similes and both of them reveal the unique imaginative power of Kālidāsa. But they do something more spectacular than that. They transport you back to that primeval sacred poetry, that foundational source, where these metaphors had arisen for the first time and which is the ever-active source of the river. Let us try to peep into that source.

Someone made a door, penetrated the rock-like gem with a thunderbolt. But, that became possible only when the ancestral poet first forged these metaphors in the smithy of his own soul. That speech itself is a door; that speech can become an avenue of entrance into or exit from somewhere; that speech has an inherent thunderbolt-like energy which can penetrate and build a path through that impenetrable stuff which conceals a solar light within itself; that the path-finding power of speech can thus remove the obstruction and release that imprisoned light. Haven't we already witnessed how both these similes were conceived and used several times in Ṛg Veda and how through repeated use they had come to acquire the state of permanent symbols there? "Agni is the great opener of doors", "the goddess dawn comes scattering light to open all the shining doors of the granite darkness,"..." Indra opened all the doors of the impenetrable fortress of the demon vale",..." It was he who opened gates in all directions for releasing the imprisoned waters",..." Goddess Dawn cut doors though that hard rock in which the Panis had concealed the resplendent rays, the cows." At one place we find sage Vaśiṣṭha telling Saraswatī—"this Vaśīṣṭha has opened the doors of *Ṛta* for you." At another, we hear, "the primal poets have opened the doors of our mind." What kind of doors are these to which the *Ṛg Veda* is so persistently alluding? A door is after all that, through which we enter the interior of a building and it is again a door which lets us out into the open. There is something inside concealed and constricted which has to be brought into the open space; there is some treasure hidden somewhere deep within, which we have to reach and find. The door is thus a metaphor which seeks to bring to light some mysterious element or fact of our life. That's why the Vedic seers have imagined the 'door' as a god, as a divine element. Thus we find Ṛṣi Gṛtsamad offering this prayer: "Let these door-goddesses whom we invoke with folded hands open fully, so that we may be enabled to come and go smoothly."

Now, let us look at the metaphor of the speech as door. What is meant here? Door for speech to enter? Door built by speech? or door made of speech? Obviously all the three meanings are inherent in this compound word, *'vāgdwāra'*. Now, the examples cited from the *Ṛg Veda* above convey a very distinct motif: breaking through an impenetrable density enabling us to have access to the inaccessible, releasing someone who is imprisoned. The two principal *Ṛg Vedic* myths of Vala and Vṛtra and the metaphors used in them clearly point towards this. The simile used by Kālidāsa in the opening verse of *Raghuvaṃśa* is thus clearly related to these myths. Where the Veda uses words like mountain, hill, or rock, Kālidāsa uses the word '*maṇi*', that is, a diamond or precious gem which agrees well with his aesthetic predilections and which, after all is no less hard or impenetrable than the Vedic 'rock'. This second metaphor of rock also can be found in several places in *Ṛg Veda*. For instance, "Indra broke that stupendous and extensive mountain into pieces with his thunderbolt and released the waters that were bound in it." Then there is Sage Parāśara telling us—"Our ancestors, the Angirasas, broke the super-hard hill with the mere sound of their utterance and built a pathway for us to reach the great realm of light." There is no dearth of such examples of the use of this metaphor as well. The whole of *Ṛg Veda* is replete with them. The word 'go' meaning cow is used throughout in the Veda in the double sense of a ray of light and speech. Even where they are not synonymous, they are wedded to each other like word and meaning, like Indra and Soma or like Soma and Agni.

Thus both these similes of Kālidāsa carry us straightway into that cluster of metaphors which is the primeval creation of Indian poetry and the origin, the fountainhead of our cultural heritage. In fact if we delve deep into some other similes used by Kālidāsa, we make the startling discovery that most of them have clearly discernible Vedic connections: they bring to our minds either the Vedic Agni or the Vedic Soma. For example, the marriage of Śiva and Pārvati has been compared in *Raghuvaṁśa* to the marriage of word and meaning. For a deep reader of Vedic poetry and its symbolism, the connection is obvious: how Pārvati is linked to Agni and Śiva to Soma and, how, their union is commemorative of the union of Soma and Agni in the *Ṛg Veda*.

Only connect: this then seems to be the golden rule to be followed in reading ancient Indian poetry so as to have our own present illumined by the experience. Could we now move from this poetry to its poetics—to a study of the criteria proper to itself? That indeed is the subject of our next lecture.

Towards a Philosophy of Imagination :

The poet is like Prajāpati, from whose will this world arises. For the poet is endowed with a power to create wondrous and unheard-of things. This power arises from the grace of Parā Vāc, which is just another name for poetic imagination (Pratibhā) which has its seat in the poet's own heart, and which is eternally in creative motion (Udita).

–Abhinavabhāratī.

Pure aesthetic experience is theirs in whom the knowledge of ideal beauty is innate; it is known intuitively, in intellectual ecstasy without accompaniment of ideation, at the highest level of conscious being; born of one mother with the vision of god, its life is as it were a flash of blinding light of transmundane origin, impossible to analyze, and yet in the image of our very being.

–Sāhitya Darpaṇa, III, 2-3

Hints from Indian Aesthetics

I

"Beauty is Truth, Truth is Beauty"—is that just romantic wishful thinking—just a cry of the heart's desire—and not a fact of mind? 'What the imagination seizes as beautiful must be true'—isn't that the kind of assertion even artists and poets of the calibre of a Tolstoy or a T.S. Eliot in our times could hardly be expected to make or even defend? How is it then that a spiritually grounded civilisation like that of India could dare describe Ultimate Reality itself in terms which are linked to Beauty rather than Truth? Truth has often been equated with 'Rasa', that is, with the very essence of aesthetic experience, or with the spirit of Delight: 'Raso Vai Saḥ' or 'Ānandam Brahma' are statements not from any text-book on poetics but from the Upaniṣads themselves.

'The poet is like Prajāpati'—as Abhinavagupta, an authority in Indian aesthetics tells us. And he is no mere aesthete, but a philosopher and a mystic in his own right. The poet's power, he tells us, arises from the grace of *Parā Vāc* i.e., the highest speech associated with the highest reality. He then goes on to equate it with *Pratibhā* (poetic imagination) which has its seat in the poet's own heart. Here we can remember the special knowledge called *'pratismṛti'* taught by Vyāsa to Yudhiṣṭhira—which was a sacred word with the potency of making things manifest and disclose their real nature. To my mind, these two things must go together: wherever there is Pratibhā, that is, Imagination of a high order, *'pratismṛti'* or the power of making things manifest and disclose their real nature is bound to accompany it. According to Vedic belief, you will recall, the world is created by Divine Consciousness in conformity with the Unmanifest, archetypal eternal truth (*Ṛta*) which is seated in the highest heaven. The Divine Power or God is thus the real poet and the world constitutes his poetry. *'Devasya paśya kāvyam, na mamār, na jīryati*—declares the *Ṛg veda*: "Look at the poetry of the Divine Power, which knows no decay or death." Obviously, in this view of things, the material world is experienced as the reflection of a divine world and therefore all the objects in this created world must posses an inherent symbolism. Platonic tradition points exactly the same way. But that tradition, as we know, has hardly any place for imagination as a legitimate mode of approaching truth. *'Pratibhā'* from the Vedic point of view, may well be an illumination of the human consciousness which corresponds to the Heavenly Light; *Pratismṛti* again, as an invocation of and a request to the gods to approach may well have been considered an inherent property of the sacred word. But, the Platonic ideal is inaccessible to both: it is the prerogative of reason and reason alone. Poets are suspect because they have the Muses' madness in their souls; and hence, the faculty called imagination can never be a reliable guide to the truth of things; salvation lies in reason alone.

But, if truth is held to be a matter of reason and reason-based principles, it is displaced from the realm of experience and expression and becomes a matter of knowledge. Now, what we call Vedic literature as a whole certainly has a place for this purely philosophical approach too, which you find worked out in all seriousness in Post-Vedic prose. But, it is necessary first of all to explore the experience where the spiritual root of this knowledge lies. Vedic hymns themselves constitute the authentic expression of spiritual experience. That's why their words and the order of the words cannot be changed. No such prohibitions operate in the case of Smṛti literature as distinguished from Śruti literature. The Vedic hymns have a multi-layered suggestivity which is the hallmark of all great poetry and the gods they are addressed to symbolise the highest values reflected in worshipful consciousness. The Vedic concept of beauty, as we have already observed, comprehends intellectual and moral values. It is this spiritual tradition which is reflected again through the various changes of cultural context in the epics, in the puraṇas, in the āgamās and in the bhakti poetry. Texts as diverse as *Bhāgavatapurāṇa Yogavāśiṣṭha, Rāmacaritamānasa* and the songs of the siddhas and saints exemplify this integrated co existence and cooperation of beauty and truth.

The problem , thus, is to avoid the displacement of truth from the realm of experience and expression. After all, how do we cognise objects? At the root of all our concepts, does not there lie the unity of subjective consciousness? It is self-awareness that precedes and is the basis of our awareness of objects. Self-awareness is the root-basis of experience and even through all objective cognition this self-awareness is continually seeking itself. Now, this consciousness has an innate ability to apprehend meaning and to express itself: it therefore must possess an original capacity of apprehending signs and symbols and of constructing them.[1] Without such original power of consciousness, no linguistic-symbolic system could have come into existence. Nor is the endless adventure of the human will to know possible without this power because an unbroken relationship between knowledge and speech is evident throughout in human consciousness. That explains why in the Indian tradition, this inherent symbol-making power of consciousness was so early defined and deified as *Vāc* (speech). Now, since this *'Vāc'* is the power of consciousness to present itself as meaning, the whole of

1. Prof. G.C. Pande is most illuminating on this subject. The interested reader can read the chapter called 'Anubhūti and Abhivyakti' in his book called '*Bhārutīya Paramparā Ke Mūl Swara*' in Hindi. His '*Bhakti-Darśana Vimarṣah*'—originally written in Sanskrit and published by the Sanskrit University, Varanasi, is a seminal text on the philosophy of Bhakti.

creation turns out to be nothing but expression. Those who find it philosophically inconvenient to accept this power as inherent and active in the consciousness are compelled to call it *Māyā-Śakti* (the power of illusion). This happened in the post-vedic period and the real breakthrough, so far as aesthetics was concerned, came only with Abhinavagupta, who, availing himself of *Saivāgam* philosophy once again restored expressive will to the static and passive Absolute.

The symbols operating in literature and the arts protect these very expressive values in a special way. If culture is awareness of values, literature is its most expressive and most powerful language. Here lies the real importance and the real justification of art and literature. They demonstrate the fundamental unity of experience and expression in the consciousness in the most self-evident manner. But this unity and its value as truth and beauty combined can be illustrated from other areas of human experience which are not necessarily aesthetic. In the course of a very illuminating discussion on this theme ('experience and expression') Prof. G.C. Pande cites the examples of Helen Keller. The way she grasped the mere touch of the name being conveyed to her simultaneously with the sensation of water falling on her hand is a demonstration—Prof. Pande says—of the fact that her mind had the innate capacity to respond to a sign without having been told anything about it. What is most significant about the experience is the extraordinary elation she felt at that moment. A particular sensation became for her simultaneously the signifier of a meaning as well as the expression of a unique experience. It shows, according to Prof. Pande, that, "communion with one's own self constitutes the fundamental original experience in which self-expression occurs for the sake of the self."[2]

It is this intuitive knowledge which would appear to have determined the nature and the special quest of Indian poetry

2. Ibid.

and poetics. It is not the exploration of the historical forms of man but the quest for this eternal form. Neither the depiction of a stable society with its secure assumptions like the classical tradition characterizes it, nor, by way of reaction and revolt the swing to a depiction of personal feelings like the Romantic movement. It is distinguished on the whole by what can only be called the expression of spiritual experience. Mainstream Indian literature is not characterized by a historical or scientific curiosity about the natural or the social reality; its distinctive tone and temper—its very flavour—is determined by the meditation on the highest ends of human life through traditionally recognisable forms. We have already had some glimpses of this literature in its various phases. It would be worthwhile now to consider the criteria proper to itself that were evolved by it in the course of its development and to consider whether and how far it has a wider resonance and applicability.

II

Sāhityaśāstra in its broadest meaning embraces the knowledge of all poetic art, be it poetry for the eye (dṛśyakāvya) or poetry for the ear *(śravyakāvya)*. It concerns itself as much with the sensitivity of the recipient *(sahṛdaya)* as with the generator and the genesis of aesthetic experience. The concept of '*sahṛdaya*' itself is crucial to Indian aesthetics. To be a '*sahṛdaya*' is to become surcharged with an overpowering longing for ideal beauty and to be capable of that 'paryutsukībhāva', which is a total displacement of the person in time and space and his transportation to an aesthetic time and space. The aesthetic experience is thus something more than aesthetic experience: it is a kind of rebirth, a temporary annihilation of the limited self. Another word for *sahṛdaya* is '*rasika*'—literally, he, who has impeccable 'taste', who can enjoy the unique flavour ('rasa') of a work of art. The preamble of the text of *Śrimadbhāgavata* invokes this concept of the '*rasika*'. Rasikas are there invited to partake of the juice that is the essence of the fruit of the tree of Vedic knowledge.

Almost all the seminal ideas which came to be developed in Indian aesthetics can be found in Bharata's *Nāṭyaśāstra*—a work concerned not with 'Ars Poetica' as such, but with dramaturgy and allied topics. The impact of this text (written sometime between the 2nd century B.C. to 2nd century A.D.) was such that for nearly two thousand years no discussion on the arts could take place outside the parameters of the *Rasa-sūtra* presented in it. The author's assertion that he is creating a 'fifth veda' which will be accessible to all castes and classes means a very radical departure from the prevailing social hierarchy. However, as Dr. Kapilā Vatsyāyāna, in her most recent and very perceptive commentary on this text has rightly observed, "inspite of this departure, Bharata shares a world-view which is reflected in the Upaniṣads and is articulated in a large body of literature including the epics."[3] Let us try to grasp the notion of 'rasa' which continues to be vitally relevant to Indian music and dance right upto the present.

According to Bharata, the primary material of '*rasa*' was *sthāyībhāva* or one of the basic instinctive attitudes like, say, love. When such an attitude found a suitable objective correlative—a person and a situation—we get the combination of *bhāva* with *vibhāva*, which was then developed through the emergence of transient feelings (*vyabhichārībhāva*) and body language that is *anubhāvas.* It is through the coming together of these universal primary emotions, their determinants and stimulants, that a state of '*rasa*' is evoked or created *(vibhāvānubhāvavyabhichārī samyogāt rasa-niṣpattiḥ).* '*Rasa*' is the net result of the process because it is āsvādya (enjoyable). Just as out of different ingredients a tasty dish may be produced, so rasas are produced out of *bhāvas* in drama. The crucial term in Bharata's formula was '*niṣpatti*'. But whether it referred to actual causation or to imitation on

3. Kapila Vatsyayan, BHARATA: The Nāṭyaśāstra, Sahitya Akademy, Delhi, p.21.

the stage or to evocation by dramatic means was far from clear. Lollata explained *'niṣpatti'* as production or causation. *Rasa* according to him is the arousal and continuity of some basic emotional attitude in real life. This view apparently failed to do justice to the distinct character of aesthetic experience. Another commentator Śaṇkuka, therefore, suggested that *'rasa'* should be regarded as the spectator's inferential awareness of the feelings imitated by the actors. Bhattanāyaka extends the rasa-theory beyond drama to poetry. He introduces the vital idea of *Sādhāraṇīkaraṇa* (universalization) and holds that '*rasa*' is a function of words or dramatic presentation which create a state of universalized or de-individualized subjectivity in the spectator or reader. Rasa in his view has several roots—feelings, generalizing effect of representation and an inward tranquillity. What poetry or drama does is to transfigure feelings so that the self is enabled to turn inward.[4]

This was certainly an improvement on the earlier views. But the real break-through was provided by Abhinavgupta. *Bhava* has to be distinguished from *rasa*. *Bhāvas* are innate tendencies while '*rasa*' is the self-enjoyment of consciousness. *Bhāva* is not produced as a psychic fact, it is only expressed as a meaning. Words present the images of the objective correlates of instinctive attitudes and their recognition evokes feelings. When this felt experience is impersonal but vivid and coherent intuition, the innate self-enjoyment of consciousness is manifested. This is revelation of consciousness.[5] Panditrāja Jagannātha goes even further and says that the absorption of consciousness in a world of felt images produces as in a dream, a state of immediacy, in which consciousness and feelings both stand revealed in an integral moment. This is a moment of great significance in which the self reveals itself in and through the limitation of feelings.

---

4. See the chapter on 'Literature' in 'Foundations of Indian Culture' by Prof. G.C. Pande, p. 279.
5. Ibid., p. 280.

This ecstatic self-revelation of consciousness in *rasānubhūti* is distinguished from the yogic *samādhi* which results from silencing the mind. *Rasānubhūti*, on the other hand, is achieved through feelings and images and not by their extinction. '*Rasa*' is thus the moment of self-revelation within a process of felt, imaginative experience evoked by words or representations: *'Ratyādyavacchinna bhagnāvarana chideva rasah.'*

One can see that the connexion of the classification of rasas (*Śṛngāra*, *Raudra*, *Vīra*, *Vībhatsa* etc.) with such a deep theory of '*rasa*' is tenuous indeed. But the connection of '*dhvani*' with '*rasa*' is another matter altogether. The issue of specificities and universalization had already been brought up and the seminal idea of *Sādhāraṇīkaraṇa* introduced into the current view that words have two types of power—one, of denotation (*abhidhā*) and the other of indication (*lakṣaṇā*). Now, a third power was aded—that of *vyanjanā* (suggestion), which is closest to the complex idea of *'dhvani'*. Ānandavardhana introduces the relation that exists between the meaning of the word and the meaning of the sentence to explain the relation between the expressed and the suggested and asserts that just as after comprehension of the sentential meaning, the meanings of individual words are not traced separately, similarly after the emergence of the suggested meaning, the expressed does not retain its seperate existence and both conjointly constitute the content of a single aesthetic experience. Abhinavagupta, thereafter, combines *'rasa'* and *'dhvani'* and welds them together in a philosophic unity. He combined within himself the experience of a mystic and the incisiveness of a philosopher. Deeply versed in *kāśmīra śaivism*, he self-consciously extends and applies his philosophic principles to the field of aesthetics.

According to *kāśmīra śaivism*, the absolute is not only self-luminous and quite like Vedāntic Brahma, but also self-conscious and dynamic. These two aspects of Ultimate Reality—self-luminosity (*śiva* or *prakāśa*) and self-consciousness (*śakti* or *vimarśa*) are best understood through the image and concept of '*ardhanārīśvara*'—i.e., male and female conjoined—the one as two and inseparable. The entire world of experience is the manifestation of absolute free-will which is the Ultimate Reality in *kāśmīr śaivism*. Consciousness is thus the capacity of awareness of the self, called *Śakti*. The aesthetic experience from this standpoint, is not based on objective perception but is a subjective experience and realization. Now, according to *Taittirīya Upaniṣad*, "He verily is 'rasa'." (*Raso vai sah*). The Ultimate Reality here has been perceived as unconditioned, inexhaustible bliss. For Abhinavagupta and Vishwanātha too, the nature of aesthetic experience is *alaukika* (trans-mundane) and akin to *brahmānanda* (i.e., mystical experience). Śaiva philosophy speaks of three kinds of impurities, namely (1) innate ignorance, concealing the real universal nature of the soul, associating the ever-free self with the creations of *māyā* (2) the psycho-physical limitation, where the self is in bondage to time, cause-effect, passions; and, (3)objective factual knowledge. In order to remove these impurities or limitations, *sādhanā* or discipline is required. If the purified state in life ideally is that of Śiva, in art the purified state of undifferentiated experience is '*rasa*' or *ānanda*. The artistic process is thus analogous to movement from impurity to purity, from grossness to subtlety, from individualism to universality, from multiplicity to unity.

It would be pertinent here to note Abhinavagupta's insistence on *Śānta rasa* (peace, tranquillity) being not just another *rasa* but the central one which permeates everything else and to which, indeed all else in drama moves. *'Hṛdayaviśrānti'* (repose), as described by Abhinava as the end of art here, would seem to be a much higher achievement of artistic endeavour than Aristotle's Catharsis. This is what Abhinava has to tell us about the artist and the spectator:

"The artistic expression is the direct expression of a feeling of passion generalised—that is, freed from distinctions in time or space and, therefore from individual and practical interest through an inner force of creative intuition within the artist. This state of consciousness ('*rasa*') embodied in the poem is transferred to the actor, the dancer, the spectator. Born in the heart of the poet, it flowers as it were in the actor and bears fruit in the spectator.

If the artist or poet has the creative intuition, the reader or spectator is the emotionally educated man, in whom lie dormant the different states of being and when he sees them manifested, he is lifted to that ultimate state of bliss, known as *ānanda*.[6]

III

Here then, is a philosophy of imagination which gives almost equal importance to the creator, the creative process and the *sahṛdaya* reader or sepctator and makes all the constituents of creativity cohere in an integrated unity. It is very difficult—almost impossible—to translate the word '*rasa*' adequately into a European language, because the concept itself is somewhat alien to mainstream western thought. The Upaniṣads, as we noted earlier, describe the supreme goal of human attainment itself as '*Rasa*'. This perception of Beauty as Truth and Truth as Beauty is by no means self-evident to philosophy eastern or western. But poets and mystics in both hemispheres have spoken of such an experience and Indian philosophy in its openness to mystical as well as poetic experience has sometimes come very close to it. We can catch glimpses of it in Vedic hymns and there are hints scattered through most of the Upaniṣads which, like the chapter X called '*Vibhūtiyoga*' in the *Gītā*, enjoin that God as '*Rasa*' must be sought out in terms of sight, hearing, meditation and union. There have been serious attempts even in contemporary

6. Abhinavabhārati, (translated by Kapila Vatsyayan).

Indian philosophy to demonstrate logically that "art seeks to delve into the truth of subjectivity and that is its primary concern, not beauty. Even when an artist seems intent on beauty, his real aim is not the creation of beauty, but to bring out the meaning of beauty."[7] A problem may, nevertheless arise. If art-experience or, 'rasa' is a mere temporary migration from our narrow self, as even Abhinava in his all-out endeavour to exalt it to the highest place would seem to imply, how could it be equated with or even compared to yogic self-realisation or mystical communion? At best, it can be a moment of self-revelation and not of true enlightenment. Hasn't Robbert Frost, for example, called it 'a momentary stay against confusion'?

On the other hand, if there is such an unbridgeable gulf between aesthetic experience and genuine mystical experience, what are we to make of such Vedic-Upaniṣadic phrases as *'raso vai sah'* and 'all-fragrant, all-relish Brahman' who is identical with Self or Atman? There are two kinds of devotees according to the *Gītā*: those who worship the Unmanifest, indefinable and changeless and those who worship the Manifest. It states very clearly that "the Unmanifest is very difficult for embodied souls to realize."[8] That is why we find in the *Gītā*, as well as in the Upaniṣads, not only the abstract notion of an Absolute who is merely the Beyond (*Parātpara*) but also of a God who is 'the father, the mother, the friend and the sustainer of the world' (Gītā IX, 17-18)—a conception answering the need of the human heart, the need for love and beauty and for work and worship. Apart from that, even a great yogi and mystic does not dwell continuously in the state of complete absorption. He too returns to normal consciousness although the illumination experienced in the transcendental state will not leave him.

7. Yashdeo Shalya, Mūlya Tattva Mimāmsā, p. 101.
8. Cf. Yeats's famous last statement: 'Man can embody truth, but he cannot ḳnow it'.

Ever since Aristotle said so in his 'Poetics', critics have gone on repeating that tragedy is the highest form of literary art. One wonders what Aristotle would have thought of our epics or even of Ānandavardhan's statement that '*The Mahābhārata* is a great epic because it teaches man to renounce the vanity of earthly glories and attain truth, eternal peace and salvation.' *Śānta rasa*, according to him, is by no means a mere negative sense of waste and emptiness, but a positive and enriching state of mind. And, is there really nothing higher even in terms of aesthetic value than Catharsis? Kālidāsa's *Śākuntala'* and Shakespeare's '*The Tempest*' alone should suffice to reveal the inadequacy of such criteria of literary excellence—what to speak of epics like *Rāmāyana* and *Mahābhārata*. Incidentally, no two epics produced by the same culture could be so divergent in tone and temper and yet both of them produce *rasānubhūti* of the same order, although the former is characterised by *Karuṇa* rasa and the latter by *Śānta rasa*.

So, how are we going to respond to this non-European way of looking at art or to its understanding and valuation of what is called creative imagination (*Kārayitrīpratibhā*, as the Sanskṛt aestheticians prefer to call it, distinguishing it from that imaginative power in the reader for which their term is *bhāvayitrī pratibhā*)? As we saw yesterday, '*rasa*' mistranslated as sentiment is manifested in terms of experience, but is really a quality belonging to the spirit. The intuition of '*rasa*' is nothing except a self-realisation in terms of imaginative experience. That would mean that imaginative experience is a legitimate mode of approaching reality and not the imitation of an imitation as Plato suspected it to be. Nor would such a philosophy of imagination get along with T.S. Eliot's later characterisation of poetry as only 'a superior form of amusement'. If poetry, or any other art is in fact capable of giving us some sort of self-realisation in terms of imaginative experience, as Rasa theory claims it does, it should suffice to show the weakness of such viewpoints and to accord it a higher place in our scheme of values.

Since it is an empirical self-realisation in imagination, 'rasa' may present itself as the essence of the most diverse characters, situations and responses, as we actually find in the reading experience of our epics. What is it after all, that literature seeks to communicate? If literature is to be something more than mere imitation of reality or a superior kind of amusement, it must communicate felt and intuited values. Now, the four categories of human endeavour in the Indian system of values do constitute a hierarchy, but there is no irreconcilable conflict between body and spirit or between desire (*kāma*) and higher aspiration (*dharma*). We have already familiarised ourselves with the Vedic image of God as the Supreme Poet, and of the human poet as his representative on earth. We have also taken cognizance of the Upaniṣadic image of two birds sitting on the same tree of life—one tasting the fruit of it and the other simply witnessing its companion. Both belong to consciousness but represent different levels of it. The one who is content to remain mere eater is also partaking of '*rasa*', but of a lower order. The one who possesses more self-consciousness and is capable of an inner freedom from desire and its objects is certainly on a higher scale. Now, it is the peculiar prerogative of the poet to connect these two poles in the most urgent and existentially meaningful way. On the one hand, he is rooted in the concrete particulars of existence and on the other hand, he is able to create significant patterns out of this experience of these particulars: patterns of involvement and liberation, of constriction and fulfilment. "The very things that ensnare man can be turned into the most potent means for his liberation"[9]—as the philosophy of the Tantra emphatically declares. Now, what is it that ensnares man and obstructs his innate freedom? Surely, limitations and distortions

9. Dr. Kapila Vatsyayan, op.cit., p. 26.

which are imposed upon him by his senses, by his mind and his instinctive impulses. But, then, these are the very materials a poet's creative imagination is supposed to be working with. So, creative imagination in its own way can and does help man to see through the various entanglements of his human condition—the various impediments to the possibility of full freedom, of self-realisation. Aristotle did his best to rescue imagination from the Platonic charge that it falsifies reality. But his own views, as we can see, don't quite lead up to a fully satisfying philosophy of imagination. Could *Rasa-dhvani* theory built over a millennium of aesthetic-philosophical thinking contribute something towards fulfilling this urgent need?

'The moment of self-surrender within a process of felt imaginative experience evoked by words or representations'—that is the minimal definition of '*rasa*'. The history of Indian arts shows the universal applicability of this theory of '*rasa*' in all the arts. Bharata's '*Nātyaśāstra*' had propounded '*rasa*' in the context of theatre and theatre in itself was to him an all-inclusive category. In Bharata's time the arts of poetry, drama, dance, music, painting and sculpture were seen to be inter-related. We have observed how the aesthetic categories were applied later to poetry and literature in their autonomous genres and how Ānandavardhana and Abhinavagupta consolidated all the accumulated ideas and fused them with their own philosophical and mystical insights to systematise everything into a unified whole—reducing everything to a single intensity. *Rasa-dhvani* theory as developed by them and reinforced by Panditarāja Jagannātha, is flexible enough to enable us to appreciate Vedic as well as classical poetry, epics like *Mahābhārata* as well as plays like *Śākuntala* and '*The Tempest*'. What enabled these aestheticians to up-date *rasa* theory and give it depth and subtlety was a novel insight into the suggestive powers of language (*dhvani siddhānta*) as well as the philosophy of

Kāśmīra Śaivism. The Śaiva God is virtually an artist who expresses himself in the form of the world and transforms himself into a 'character' to play a role but is always free to recall his true nature and enjoy the world as a creative spectator. It is the essential nature of the Absolute Will, according to Śaivāgama doctrine, to manifest itself just as it is the sun's essential nature to shine and send forth rays. Now, experience and consciousness imply a 'self' and, therefore, the Absolute is both self-luminous (*Śiva* or *Prakāśa*) and self-consciousness (*Śakti* or *Vimarśa*). There can be no consciousness without self and no self without consciousness. Consciousness is, thus, the capacity of self-awareness which is called 'Śakti'. It was this central philosophical principle which led Abhinavagupta to re-interpret the nature of aesthetic experience. The aesthetic experience is *ānanda*. It is self-luminous and self-conscious, devoid of all duality; it emerges from a single unified source which has the potency of multiplicity. The aesthetic experience is thus different from ordinary experience as it is not based on objective perception but is a subjective experience and analogous to mystic experience. It is in this context that the word *camatkāra* (a flash of lightening) is applied to the realm of aesthetics. Abhinavagupta develops its aesthetic implications and says that *camatkara* is the sudden increase of consciousness of the self which is free from limitations. This is what produces *ānanda*. Here he incorporates Bhattanāyaka's term *Sādhāraṇīkaraṇa* (universalization) to explain the freedom from limitation which is achieved in aesthetic experience.

Finally, in the fifteenth century, there appear two exponents of Gauḍīya Vaiṣṇavism, who extend the scope of *rasa* and *rasāsvāda* to the realm of *bhakti*. Abhinavagupta had availed himself of a philosophical tradition to interpret *rasa*. The Gosvamis, interestingly, employ poetry and the concept of *rasa* to evolve a full-fledged theory of *bhakti rasa*. *Ujjvalnīlamaṇī and Bhaktirasāmṛtsindhu*, the two famous texts by these extraordinary men provide a fresh insight into the nature and scope of aesthetic experience. Their key-word, of course, is surrender. The point to be kept in mind, as Dr. Kapila Vatsyayana has observed, is that "Indian art is not religious in the ordinary sense, nor is there a theology of aesthetics, but the two fields interpenetrate because they share a basic world-view in general and the specific goal of *Mokṣa* or liberation in particular. After all, the art seeks to communicate primarily felt and intuited values and do it through the representation of experience in suitable form. And in the Indian hierarchy of values, *mokṣa* or freedom from bondage was and is the highest value. Here is, then a theory of art, which to quote Dr. Vatsyayana again, "can be clearly distinguished from Aristotle or subsequent theories of aesthetics and art in the post-renaissance west." Bharata's *rasa* or its more philosophically evolved form propounded by Ānandavardhana and Abhinavagupta together (with the perfect definition of *rasāsvāda* given by *Viśvanātha* in *Sāhitya Darpaṇa* quoted at the very outset) can thus be looked upon as a philosophy of imagination. It is only to be hoped that somebody some day will go deeper into its relevance and reveal its secret but sure affinity with the insights of such western masters as Meister Eckhart, William Blake and W.B. Yeats. We invoke these names just to remind ourselves that the theory of *Rasa-dhvani* as originally propounded by Bharata and later perfected by Abhinavagupta transcends the cultural specificity of India despite its being firmly rooted in the specific culture. Infact, Ānanda Coomaraśvāmy's pioneering initiative in this direction is, I hope, too well-known to be discussed here. Still, by way of a brief reminder and as a befitting conclusion to this lecture, I would like to quote Coomarasvāmy's own words—words which happen to form the conclusion of his famous essay on 'The Theory of Art in Asia':

> "The Indian theory, in origins and formulation, seems at first sight to be *sui generis*. But merely because of the

specific idiomatic and mythical form in which it finds expression, it need not be thought of as otherwise than universal. It does not in fact differ from what is implicit in the far eastern view of art, or in any essentials from the scholastic Christian point of view, or what is asserted in the aphorism of Blake; it does differ essentially from the modern non-intellectual interpretations of art as sensation."[10]

10. Ananda Coomaraswamy, Transformation of Nature in Art., p. 56-57.

Bhakti Poetry :

"This that thou now seest is My Supreme Shape, My form of luminous energy, the universal which none but thou amongst men has as yet seen. It is an image of my very self figured in cosmic existence and the soul in perfect union with me sees it without any bewilderment..., but since the lower nature in thee is not yet prepared to look upon it with that strength and tranquility, I will reassume again for thee my Nārāyaṇa figure in which the human mind sees toned to its humanity the calm helpfulness and delight of a friendly Godhead. The greater form is only for the rare, highest souls, The gods themselves ever desire to look upon it. It cannot be won by Veda or austerities or sacrifice, it can be seen, known, entered into only by that Bhakti which regards, adores and loves me alone in all things."

–Śrī Aurobindo's trans. of *Gītā*, chapter XI.
Essays on the Gītā, p. 379-80.

"...The phrase 'religion of experience' has two distinct and mutually incompatible meanings. There is the experience of which the Perennial Philosophy treats—the direct apprehension of the divine Ground in an act of intuition possible only to the selflessly pure in heart. And there is the experience induced by revivalist sermons, impressive ceremonials, or the deliberate efforts of one's own imagination. This 'experience' is a state of emotional excitement....But emotional excitement....is always excitement of that individualised self, which must be died to by anyone who aspires to live to divine reality..."

–Aldous Huxley, *The Perennial Philosophy*, p. 261

Background and Prespective

I

'Bhakti' literally means division or separation: hence the connotation of an intense awareness of separation from the Ground—The Unity of Being—and an equally intense longing for re-integration with it. The *Bhagavad Gītā* itself, the arch text of Vaiṣṇavism or of the Bhāgavata religion, teaches *Bhakti-Yoga* as the highest mode of joining man to Deity. Arjuna earlier, had been asked by his Divine friend to sink his separate personality in the Impersonal Self. But now he is confronted with the vision of Universal Godhead and commanded to seek oneness with him by knowledge, works and adoration, Arjuna is perplexed. "Thou art the supreme source of all beings"—he says—"a presence pervading the universe with thy forms, a person manifest in creatures and in Nature and in our hearts by Thy mighty world-Yoga. As such I must know, adore, unite myself with thee in all my being, consciousness, thoughts, feelings and actions. But what then of the immutable you spoke of—who never manifests, enters into no relation with the universe, is eternally silent, impersonal and immobile?" To this question Kṛṣṇa replies with a resounding firmness, "Those who found their mind in Me and by constant union seek after me with supreme faith, I hold to be the most perfectly in union of yoga." This supreme faith is that which sees god in all. Worship of the relationless Unmanifest Absolute also is equally valid and fruitful but it is extremely arduous. Kṛṣṇa recommends the full and natural movement of the spiritualised human nature towards Puruṣottam (the Supreme Person), as the direct and the best way for embodied creatures. That, indeed is *Bhakti*.

Before we start talking about the mediaeval *Bhakti*-poetry, it would be necessary to establish the background of this literature in classical and post-classical Sanskṛt itself. For a long time, as we have already seen in the course of our last lecture, *Bhakti* or love of God was not recognised as a *rasa* by rhetoricians; but after the great *Bhāgavata Purāṇa*, one of the central texts of Hindu religious life and the basic scripture of the *Bhakti* religiousness in all its Vaiṣṇava varieties composed about the eighth century, such a title could not justly be denied to *Bhakti*. The *Gītagovinda* of Jayadeva—with which, I am told, you are already familiar in translation—had to be recognized as a perfect blending of *Bhakti* and *Śṛngāra* in lyrical form. This series of songs depicting the various stages of love between Rādhā and Kṛṣṇa is unique for its sonorous quality, haunting rhythm and perfect correspondence between sense and sound. The *stotra* literature also has to be mentioned in this context—particularly because, it was composed by men who were outstanding philosophers. The *Śivamahimāstotra*, the *Soundaryalaharī* attributed to Śankarāchārya, the stotras of Abhinavagupta are some examples; where religious feeling and poetic inspiration are blended spontaneously.

And, even before *Bhāgavata*, there is the *Bhāgavad Gītā* and the Mahābhārata within which the *Gītā* text has its proper setting. Some recent scholars have expressed the opinion that 'this epic as a whole is the principal and without doubt the most ancient document of bhakti.' Vālmīki's *Rāmāyaṇa* can also be studied from this perspective. How does *bhakti* manifest itself in the midst of human living with all its stresses and strains and contradictions—that's the central question; and these epics and other narrative writings of the bhakti tradition offer a variety of answers to that question. *'Bhaktosi me sakhā ceti'*—says Kṛṣṇa to Arjuna on the battlefield of kurukṣetra. Arjuna is Kṛṣṇa's *bhakta* (devotee), his relationship with Him is that of a dear friend. Friendship, by the way, is the commonest term in the *Ṛgveda Saṁhitā* for the mutual turning towards of Man and God. *Bhakti* in the *Gītā* is a gathering together of mind, intellect and heart in their unity and turning them towards Kṛṣṇa. It is a mode of relationship with the supreme Godhead in which man's whole being is concentrated on and reaches out to Him in Bhaktiyoga.

Yet another kind of relationship with the Divine celebrated in the *Bhāgavata Purāṇa* is that of the milkmaids (gopis) of Braj. Hindi poets of the sixteenth century—Sūradāsa in particular, being the most notable amongst them—have also narrated the story about Kṛṣṇa's friend and emissary called Uddhava going to Braja and trying to make the love-lorn gopis see reason. Ironically, it is not the gopis who are convinced and converted but Uddhava, the philosopher himself, who is stunned into the realisation that loving Kṛṣṇā, as the gopis do, is the real thing, the ultimate value to be sought after, even by sages and saints. Uddhava, like Arjuna is solely devoted to Kṛṣṇa as his friend, but he is also a *muni* or thinker. What we find dramatized in this story is a moving vision of his sort of *bhakti* and understanding, transcending and fulfilling themselves in the mode of being of the gopis. Various modes of bhakti have developed in the Vaiṣṇava, Śaiva and Śākta schools. Of these, the Vaiṣṇava tradition from the Gītā to the school of Caitanya is the richest so far as it is a matter of capturing the pure essence of *bhakti* in experience, expression and literary depiction.

Most of the basic patterns or varieties of bhakti we find in the later bhakti literature proper are foreshadowed in *Rāmāyaṇa, Mahābhārata, Bhāgavatpurāṇa* and *Viṣṇupurāṇa.* Even evil characters like Śiśupāla in the *Mahābhārata* and Rāvaṇa in the *Rāmāyaṇa*—with all their hatred and bitter opposition to the Divine—have been portrayed as perverse manifestations and inversions of what is at bottom, *bhakti.* 'Hatred of God may bring the soul to God'—as one of the 'Supernatural songs' by W.B. Yeats tells us. There is Prahlāda in *Viṣṇupurāṇa,* about whom Kṛṣṇa says in the *Gītā* that among the demons, Prahlāda is an embodiment of his own essence. The story of this demon-born bhakta is found in so many texts besides *Viṣṇupurāṇa.* His bhakti in the *Viṣṇupurāṇa* is characterised as much by intensity and vividness of imagination as by its intense intellectual and ethical passion. It has nothing to do with the kind of emotionalism which has been criticised by Huxley in his 'Perennial Philosophy' (cited above). It is through meditation that he achieves unification with.God. In a memorable verse of the legend, Prahlāda prays to the Lord, "The attachment for and fixation that undiscerning people have on sense-objects may be mine always in my thinking on you."

II

Bhakti is proclaimed rather than defined in *Gītā* and *Viṣṇupurāṇa* presents before us an exemplar of ideal *bhakti* in the figure of Prahlāda. *Śrimadbhāgavata* on the other hand, presents an elaborate doctrine of the love of God. It is, in fact, the source book of all *bhakti* poets. It claims the status of a fifth *puruṣārtha* for *bhakti* and even ranks *bhakti* above *mokṣa*. The poetic portrayal of what a bhakta is, of how he thinks and feels and acts is accompanied here by reflective meditations on what *bhakti* means and what the essential nature of its object is. What we see here emerging in the forefront now is the ancient Upaniṣadic doctrine of rasa which sustains both the aesthetics and the metaphysics of the *bhakti* tradition as it subsequently developed. It is an enactment of *Adbhuta rasa*—the *rasa* of wonder—that we witness here in the *Bhāgavata* when the Lord appears out of the shattered pillar in the guise of *Nṛṣimha avatāra* (Man-lion incarnation). "The sense of the marvellous here", as Prof. J.L. Mehta has aptly remarked, "is correlated with both the nature and circumstances of the epiphany and the metaphysical-theological doctrine of the *Bhāgavata*. Even where other rasas are dramatized, there is always an enveloping sense of a marvel taking place which the poet suggests so often by prefixing an, 'O wonder of wonders' to his descripton'."[1]

1. J.L. Mehta, 'Bhakti in Philosophical Perspective', Philosophy & Religion, p.209.

It is in this way that the *Bhāgavatapurāṇa* became the basic text in which *bhakti* starts assuming that character of a rasa which corresponds to the upaniṣadic conception of Ultimate Reality itself as a *rasa* (*Raso vai saḥ*) and also to the creation of a poetic work which is designed to generate this rasa in the like-minded, 'Sahṛdaya' reader. We have already spoken of the *Mahābhārata* as a coherently organized poem; similarly the *Bhāgavata* too constitutes the supreme literary text in its style as well as structure. The *Gītā* is said to be the heart of the *Mahābhārata*; similar is the importance of the tenth book of the *Bhāgavata*, its very core. There is yet another correspondence between the Gītā and the *Bhāgavata* which invites our attention: just as the eleventh chapter of the *Gītā* presents the epiphany of Kṛṣṇa's *Viśva-rūpa-darśana* (universal form), similarly the five chapters on the rāsa (rasa as ecstatic dance) in this book of the *Bhāgavata* presents the epiphany of Kṛṣṇa as Rāsadhāri—Master of rāsa. Here we see manifested a new model of *bhakti* and a new vision of the universe and of man's life within it. Then, in the sixteenth century, we come across a third epiphany of this nature in the life of Śri Chaitanya of Bengal who, as a matter of fact, represents the culmination and fulfilment of this philosophy and religion of love. He is even today regarded as an embodied manifestation of the love of Kṛṣṇa and Rādhā and as the very incarnation of *bhakti* as *rasa*.

The *Gītā* is categorical in affirming that the worship of the personal God is superior to the contemplation of the impersonal absolute. The God of the *Gītā* is more than the *Upaniṣadic Brahman* or the *Sānkhyan Puruṣa*. He is the Supreme Person (*Puruṣottam*), other than the individual soul and insentient nature, controlling them both. He is seated in every man's heart as the inner monitor, presiding over his destiny, ready to guide him and respond to the feelings of the heart. He is the one God behind all gods. All worship ultimately goes to him alone. The human form of the personal God is the result of incarnation and the doctrine of Incarnation may be described as the main innovation of the Gītā. But his incarnation in history is not unique. He is born in every age when virtue declines and evil flourishes to protect the virtuous and destroy the evil doers and re-establish the moral order.

Besides the *Gītā* and the *Purāṇas*, one has to mention the Āgamic literature too in the context of the Bhakti movement. Āgamas or Tantras are revelations in conformity with the revelations of the Vedas. Their date is uncertain; but since Buddha was familiar with them, they are obviously pre-Buddhist. The original Tantras are divided into three main groups according as the deity chosen for worship is Vīṣṇu, Śiva or Śakti. Thus there are Vaiṣṇava Āgamas (or *Pāñcarātra*), the Śaiva Āgamas and the Śākta Āgamas, besides the later Buddhist Āgamas composed in Tibet. The Śākta group is the most popular, so much so that the word '*tantra*' has come to mean, generally though mistakenly, only Śākta Āgamas. One doctrine which is common to all of them is the notion of a pure (as distinguished from impure) creation. It implies the possibility of supernatural life, a life beyond the evils of this world. According to this doctrine, emancipation is not simply a subsidence of life and a return to the unmanifest and transcendent source of life but the gaining of an everlasting life beyond sorrow and ignorance. The implication is that spiritual reality is capable of internal differentiation and of constituting a world by emanations. It is at once consciousness and an infinity of power and potentiality. While continuing to exist in its fullness, it can also exist in partial manifestation and a hierarchy of beings. The soul subject to ignorance, passion and evil actions lives within the bounds of the imperfect and transitory natural world; but through *bhakti* may hope to enter the higher worlds of light. Pure creation, thus serves to bridge the gulf between God and Man.

As for the practice of spiritual life, the Āgamas emphasize images, temples, formal ritual along with *upāsānā*, meditation, devotion and surrender. It is in the Ālvāra saints of the south that we find, prior to the medieval *bhakti* poets, expression of an intense personal relation and feeling of love. Their songs are imperishable monuments of divine love. The Ālvāras came from diverse castes and the love of God of which they sang carried within it the possibility of a socially levelling and reforming doctrine. It was their devotional fervour which along with the doctrines of the Āgamas formed the basis of the philosophical systematization which Yāmunāchārya, Rāmānuja, Nimbārka and Vallabhāchārya completed. Among these, the philosophy of Rāmānuja (*Viśiṣṭādvaita*) was to the greatest of Bhakti poets what the philosophical system of St. Thomas Aquinas was to Dante.

III

Poetry, says Heidegger, "is the act of establishing by the word and in the word." The Supreme importance attached by the Bhakti poets to the act of Naming deserves our close attention. It is more than a mere ritualistic gesture for them; it is the very basis of the human being's relationship with the Divine. Tulasīdāsa—perhaps the greatest among the poets of this mediaeval period—the author of the famous epic *Rāmacaritamānas,* is emphatically clear about it. To name is to create. According to him, "Name and form are both attributes of God. Who can presume to settle the point of precedence between the two? We do observe, however, in our daily experience that form is subordinate to Name. Without naming a thing we hardly know or feel it intimately; but even in the absence of a thing, mere naming of it is enough to enable us to visualise and feel it. Both are without beginning, but Name is the efficient witness between the abstract (*Nirguṇa*) and the concrete (*Saguṇa*). He is the wise interpreter who illuminates both (i.e., the Absolute without attributes and the Personal God) for us."

I invite you to compare the poetic wisdom of these verses from the first canto of Tulsīḍāsa's epic poem to the existential logic of Heidegger—a philosopher, who, according to George Steiner, is "one of the deepest readers of poetry in our time."

> "Poetry is the act of establishing by the word and in the word. What is established in this manner? The permanent. But can the permanent be established then? Is it not that which has always been present? No. Even the permanent must be fixed so that it will not be carried away...The poet names the Gods and names all things in that which they are...When the poet speaks the essential word, the existent is by this naming nominated as what it is. So it becomes known as existent. Poetry is the establishing of being by means of the word."[2]

"Whatever flames upon the Night
Man's own resinous heart hath fed"

—according to a famous poem of W.B. Yeats.[3] Do we find here the metaphysical despair of the modern man in search of a soul? Or is it the inevitable gloom of a mind, which having reached the limits of post-renaissance humanism, finds himself yearning for a lost wisdom? The European renaissance, in spite of the great intellectual energy it released, inspite of the overall transformation of society that it achieved, is still supposed to have brought in its wake a certain dissociation of sensibility—the necessary spiritual price that had to be paid by the European man for the freedom from the constrictions of their own mediaeval system and for the resultant adventures of the mind. What was the character of our own medieval renaissance?

Śrimadbhāgavata—that source book of *bhatki*-poetry—claims the status of a fifth *puruṣārtha* for *bhakti* and even ranks it above them—above, even *mokṣa*. The actual realisation of this fifth *Puruṣārtha*, however, had to wait. 'Poetry is born out of humiliation'—says W.H. Auden. This remark does seem to make some sense in respect of what this great bhakti

2. Poetry, Language & Thought, Martin Heidegger, p. 2.
3. 'Two Songs from a Play', Collected Poems, p. 240.

movement could achieve during that late mediaeval period—one of the darkened periods of our long history. The movement did bring about something like a spiritual renaissance and did generate some cultural confidence that enabled our people to resist and survive the unprecedented onslaughts of what Alduous Huxley in his brilliant exposition of 'the Perennial Philosophy'—has called theological imperialism. But, in spite of an incredible burst of creative energy throughout the length and breadth of India, the movement did not and could not become an effective instrument for the regeneration of Indian society. History itself was the great adversary; the times were out of joint and under the conditions of political subjection and a degenerated aristocracy, saints and poets could hardly be expected to set them right.

Let us listen to the voice of some of these saint-poets. Is it not strange to find them using the same imagery of the Dark Night and the burning heart which we had noticed in Yeats's poem? Here is Kabīra:

> 'Whole night, the soul in its agony of separation, kept on crying like a bird separated from its mate: Kabīra burned his heart and engendered the light of passion to find a path through the darkness.'

And here is Malika Mohammad Jāyasī, introducing his epic *Padmāvata*:

> 'This, then is the whole story I have managed to put together—a story of the agony of love drenched in tears. And for putting it together, I have used the gum of my own blood.'

Let us listen to *Tulsīdāsa* now:

> Without Rāma, the city of Ayodhyā appears like the dark night of a dense forest. Men and women assume the shapes of ferocious beasts. People are mortally scared of

one another. Home looks desolate like the cremation ground; one's own family members frighten one like ghosts; friends have become the very messengers of Death, all the plants and creepers are languishing and one cannot bear to look at the ponds and rivers which are fast drying up.

And this is Mirābāi, the queen, who won't recognise her earthly husband because Kṛṣṇa alone is her Lord:

Strange, I should still be drawing my breath
Dark night of mute agony, passed in counting stars
Shall I thrust a dagger into my heart.
T'was sunset...it's now morning: he kept mute
Nor did he open the door.
We didn't exchange a word; just think of it.
He appeared in my dream, how could I know Him?
I'm plunged in bitter grief—with eyes wide open
All say He's coming, coming...but there's no trace.

These images and symbols cut across the divisions of Saguṇa and Nirguṇa Bhakti, Sūfīsm and Vaiṣṇavism, low caste and high caste. Kabīra and Jāyasī on the one hand, and Sūradāsa, Tulsīdāsa and Mirābai on the other, are alike concerned with the same agony and ecstasy of love, the same incessant churning of the inner darkness.

But what is this Dark Night and what does all this yearning and burning—this passion of self-surrender—amount to? In yet another poem, Kabīra speaks of "that earthen lamp lighted in the palace of the void, upon which a thousand suns can be sacrificed." Pandita Vidyānivāsa Miśrā—an acknowledged authority on bhakti literature has proposed a basis on which this mediaeval movement of bhakti can be distinguished from the earlier cycle of Sanskrit poetry. As we have already observed, with all these saint-poets including the Vīraśaiva poets and Ālvāra poets of the remote south, experience spoke in the mother-tongue. Pan-Indian Sanskṛt, the second language of cultured Indians for centuries had given way to the people's languages and dialects—Brajbhāṣā for Sūradāsa and Mīrābaī, Avadhī for Tulsīdāsa and colloquial Kannada and Tamil for the southern saint-poets. And many of them belonged to the privileged classes or castes. They were of every class, caste and trade; some were even outcastes and some illiterate. Moreover, this *bhakti* literature begins precisely at the point at which ancient literature ends. Ancient Sanskṛt poetry, according to Pandita Vidyânivāsa Miśrā, is the consciousness of morning or morning wisdom, whereas medieval *bhakti* poetry is the consciousness of Night—of the dark night of the soul.[4] Was this dark period, then, paradoxically, also the period of the awakening of the whole man—the man in whom lay dormant the hitherto unforeseen possibilities of an all-embracing, all-transcending love?

IV

At the beginning of the Modernist Movement in Hindi, it was the fashion in literary circles to dismiss mediaeval *bhakti* poetry as other-worldly and therefore irrelevant. The accent fell differently then. Secularism, scientific point of view, search for individuality, progressivism seemed to be the obvious values to be pursued and the medieval ethos which could still be seen operating as a source of inspiration for Hindi poets like Maithilīśaraṇa Gupta during the first quarter of this century now seemed to be quite discordant with the spirit of the Age. Most of our poets were quite understandably swept away by the humanist and anti-metaphysical trend of modernism and saw little more than a world-weary mysticism in bhakti-poetry. It was difficult for them to realise at that point of time the creative and critical implications of the cultural differences between themselves and their western counterparts. They took for granted the incompatibility of the humanist and the religious points of view, and were in the habit of erecting a barrier

4. Dr. Vidyānivāsa Mishra, Sahitya Kā Prayojana, p. 52.

between the sacred and the profane which simply was not there.

Bhakti poetry was certainly a movement from below. Most of this poetry had been produced in bhākhā, replacing and for that matter, dethroning Sanskṛt completely—raising *bhākhā* itself to the level of lingua franca and making it act as some sort of a cultural clearing house for songs composed in the regional dialects of far-flung areas of the sub-continent. Who could have foreseen lyrics and even epics of such enduring quality being created in such abundance and variety in those rustic languages which had hardly ever been thought capable of such poetic achievements? The poets themselves did not claim any literary merit for their work: there were no manifestoes, no formal declarations of a new poetics. In fact, they are self-deprecatingly modest about their aims and procedures. Thus, Tulsīdāsa states at the very beginning of his epic:

> O you creatures of the land, of water and of air ! I recognise each and everyone of you as the living embodiment of my Lord Rāma and his consort Sītā; and I bow before you all with folded hands. Here I am, longing to sing the praises of my lord: how can my petty intellect fathom that ocean? I do not see any way out. My longing is like a king, while my actual capacity is that of a pauper. Just look at this yawning gulf between my lowly mind and the loftiness of my aspirations: I am like a man, who goes vainly begging from door to door for just a cup of butter-milk and yet aspires for the elixir of the gods.[5]

Bhakti poetry is by no means a negation of life. In fact, it is a negation of all negations—a radical revaluation of the prevalent social codes and conventions. We had mentioned Kabīra and Mirābai. No two poets could be more different from each other; and yet their love of God (Kṛṣṇa for Mirābai

5. Rāmacaritamānas, Bālkānda.

and 'Rāma as the Impersonal' Absolute for Kabīra) is not only an unconditional giving up of all; it is necessarily 'anti-structure', 'anti-social', 'unruly' relationships; unmaking, undoing, the merely man-made. It is an act of violation against ordinary expected loyalties, a breakdown of the predictable and the secure. The Lord is like the illicit lover; He will break up the world of karma and normal relationships; the husband's family must necessarily be violated and trespassed against, if one should have anything to do with God. Most of these poets are actively engaged in some traditional craft for their livelihood: Kabīra is a weaver, Ravidāsa a cobbler, Nāmadeva a tailor, Sūradāsa a singer at the temple. Tulsīdāsa himself—the most conservative idealist amongst them all and a staunch defender of Vedic tradition and social order, shows utter disregard for wealth and rank and ridicules book-learning in no uncertain terms. In fact his subtle ironic undertones expose the hollowness and hypocrisy of the privileged social orders much more effectively than the overtly protestant voices. These saint-poets—Southern or Northern, Eastern or Western make use in their poetry of an accumulated stock of figures, symbols and paradoxes which are drawn from an ancient and pan-Indian pool of symbology. Whether they are the twelfth century Vacanakāras (Vīrśaivas) writing in Kannada or the Ālvāras from Tamil country, or the 16th century Vaiṣnavites of Bengal, Gujarat and the Hindi heartland, they are the great integrators, bringing the high to the low, esoteric paradox to the man in the street, transmuting ancient and abstruse ideas into live contemporary experiences. At the same time, they make us feel by finding everyday symbols for the timeless that even now the eternal design may reflect itself in sordid particulars. It was the most widespread and inter-related movement in space as well as time. Many of these poets travelled widely across the country and knew each other's mind. We have already acquainted ourselves with Kaśmīrī Śaivāgama. Isn't it astounding how Śaivism knits faraway Kaśmira with South India, and within South India the saint-poets of Tamil, Kannada and Telugu? Kabīra of the Hindi heartland gets his initiation from Rāmānanda, who had come all the way to Benaras on the Ganges from the deep South. Caitanya of Bengal was inspired by the southern school of Nimbārka. In fact, from the seventh century onward, century after century, *bhakti* movements can be seen to have grown one after another in different regions and languages, in Tamil, Kannada, Marathi, Gujarati, Hindi, Bengali, Assamese and Punjabi. It seems to have spread like a lit fuse from region to region, century to century, quickening the religious impusle.[6] Arising in particular regions, speaking the local spoken language, this poetry is yet inter-regional and through this cultural clearing house of the central *Bhākhā*—as we have already hinted above—it is both collected from and then redistributed to the four corners of the country.

It was the personal use of a more than personal idiom and symbology with its roots in ancient tradition and the general, culturally unified way of life that enabled these saint-poets to sing so gloriously and to communicate so effectively. If you study various similies and analogies which they use in their poetry, you will be astonished to recognise similarities with the imagery that you can recollect from your study of the Upaniṣads, the *Gītā* and the Pūrānas and even the works of classical Sanskṛt poets. Here are a few examples of such recurrent and widely disseminated imagery and symbology: 'the Seed and the Tree, the Sea and the Rivers, the Spider and its self-woven web, the thread and the gems, the Warp and the Woof, the River and the Boat, the Chariot and the Charioteer, the King and his Subjects, the Child and its fantasies, the Stage and Acting, the Sparks and the Anvil, the Fish and the Fisherman, the Sun and the Stars, the Lotus and the Honeybee, the Puppet and the Puppeteer, the Dream, the Dance and the Sport (*līlā*), the Swan and the Crow etc. etc. The intensity of their love and devotion towards God does not make them lose their grip on life as it is lived in the world. In fact, it tends

6. Speaking of Śiva, translated with an introduction by A.K. Ramanujan, Penguin.

to sharpen their wit and to enlarge the scope of their sympathy. Here is, for instance a couplet from '*Tulsī-Satsaī*': a minor work of Tulsīdāsa:

> "In rainy season, the cuckoo assumes silence,
> saying to herself: "This
> is the hour of the frogs. Who would care to
> remember me now?"

And, here is a song from his '*Vinaya-patrikā*'—a collection of confessional lyrics:

"Up-till now, it has been death-in-life for me. No further dying for me. By the grace of Śrī Rāma, the dark night called the world has passed away: I find myself fully awake now and am no longer going to be stung by the scorpion. The precious jewel of the Sacred Name lies safe within my heart. I won't let it slip away."

The sacred name is the precious jewel. "They do not know the secret of the name 'Rāma"—says the poet Nāmadeva in one of his songs: "The learned expound the Vedas/but silly Nāmadeva knows only Rāma". Just mark the irony implicit here. The learned are no longer in possession of the secret, which only the wisdom of the heart can bring back to life. Poets like Nāmadeva can justly lay claim to this wisdom.

> Say Rāma hear Rāma
> Do not be swept away
> by the waters of delusion
>
> That, which is beyond speech
> cannot be spoken of
> Nor written down on paper.
> Effortlessly I found
> the master of the universe.

Rāṃa is my father
Rāma is my mother
He gives life to all beings.

So says the tailor Nāmadeva
So proclaims
The *Gītā.*[7]

Whence comes this confidence that sets the saying of the humble tailor and the authority of scripture on the same footing? From experience of course, from direct perception of the divine. From the Vedic ages down through the centuries to our own day, it has been consistently claimed that the ultimate reality can be directly perceived—though never in normal consciousness." Study of the scriptures is fruitless", says the great Śankara, "so long as Brahman has not been experienced." 'He is born to no purpose' sạys Śrī Rāmakṛṣṇa, who is unable to realize God.' And God can be realized in many ways. 'Truth is one'—declares the Ṛg veda, 'but sages call it by various names.' It's hardly to be wondered at that the poet Nāmadeva addresses his Lord not only as 'Rāma' but also as Haṛi, Viṭṭhala, Gopāla, and Govinda.' Even Kabīra addresses so many of his poems to 'Rāma'.

The *bhakti*-poets sang their songs in a very responsive and memoried milieu. Even as critics of the life around them, they were immediately responded to by a traditional and devout audience. In spite of political subjugation, in spite of the deterioration of learning and creativity at the top levels of society, the oral tradition was still very much alive; and thanks to the poets themselves, who rekindled the Word through the live speech of common people, gods could still be invoked to make their presence felt in human experience. The paganism of the human heart was irrepressible and once it was rekindled by the poets, ancestral voices could once again

7. The Hindi Padāvali of NĀMADEVA, W.M. Callewaert and Mukund Lath, Motilal Banarsidass.

be heard clearly. In such a milieu, the bhakti-poet was not at all concerned about so-called self-expression. Like Bunyan he appealed to Everyman. The mask they chose was much more innately expressive and communicative than their own personal voice. Of course it was their own unmistakably unique voice whether it is Narasī Mehtā from Gujarat or Bāsavannā from Karnataka or Kabīra or Tulsīdāsa from the Hindi heartland, or Mīrābai from Rajasthan. You can not confuse them with one another even in terms of tone of voice. But the resonance comes from a deeper source. The poet becomes the medium through which the great tradition is enabled to speak. If the world created by Tulsīdāsa in his epic *Rāmacaritmānasa*, or by Sūradāsa in his *Sūrasāgara*, is the world created by imagination, then it could only be the imagination which Blake calls the Eternal Body of Man. One of the fundamental myths of India is that, which recognises the indissoluble unity of Eternal God and Eternal Man—Nara and Nārāyaṇa. The *Mahābhārata* as well as the *Gītā* emphasise this fact again and again that the relation between Arjuna and Kṛṣṇa is that of Nara and Nārāyaṇa. If Kṛṣṇa is an incarnation of Nārāyaṇa, i.e., Vishṇu, Arjuna is the incarnation of Man, that is Nara.

V

The language in which the modern Indian poets express themselves to-day is the creation of the *bhakti* poets, whether it be Bengali, Gujarati, Kannada, Punjabi or Hindi. But, owing to historical circumstances, their relationship with those not so remote ancestors, as we have already noted, has not proved to be as creatively significant as it might well have been. Our twentieth century started with two main visions or programmes of national reconstruction. One was the Tagorean dream of East-West synthesis and the other was the uncompromisingly sharp indictment by Gandhiji in *Hind Swarāja* of the modern materialistic western civilisation and a radical reaffirmation of faith in the traditional Indian way of life. Both Gandhi and

Tagore had been deeply influenced by that common source of spiritual nourishment—the medieval *Bhakti* movement. How far have we travelled from that point in our recent history where such divergent minds and sensibilities as those of Gandhi and Tagore could still converge within a common frame of reference! Is that framework still available to us? Can it still shape our response to the realities of our situation?

It is not difficult to see why these outstanding figures of modern Indian history could seek and find such glowing confirmation of their Vaiṣṇava heritage. Tagore was delighted with the joyfully creative and playful aspect of Vaiṣṇava poetry and also with the mystical songs of Kabira; while Gandhi discovered in it a deep recognition of the reality of human suffering and a means of activating our social conscience. Tagore found vindication of his own life-affirming mysticism not only in Kabīra, but also in poets like Dādu and Rajjab. "What do you see?"—people asked Rajjab, when he was reported to have received spiritual enlightenment. Tagore loved to quote the answer given by Rajjab: "I see the eternal play of life. I hear heavenly voices singing: give form to the yet unformed; speak out and express." The *Bhakti*-poets for Tagore, then, meant just this liberating energy, this capacity to counteract the debilitating effects of social rigidity. In his poetry as well as prose, we can see him deploring this very denial and distortion of life-energies leading to that 'bankruptcy of life', which Śrī Aurobindo too has underlined in his *The Life Divine.* Throughout all Tagore's writing, we discover that delight in existence, articulated in terms of a love and piety which declares its links with the Vaiṣṇava heritage. We can notice at the same time, the poet's unconcealed impatience with pedantry and rigidity. Here he was certainly at one with the medieval *bhakti* poet Narasī Mehtā of Gujarat who had found it necessary to hit hard at the hollowness of mere ritualistic gestures.

Another asset of this Vaiṣṇava heritage was a clear recognition of the reality of human suffering and a new emphasis on identifying with the sufferings of others. Why, after all should the man of God in Narasi's poem ask for a return to this world of suffering in birth after birth? (*Hari nā jana to mukti na māge, māge janamo janam avatār re*)? One explanation of it—and a very touching explanation—lies in that famous song of Narasi Mehta which haunted Mahatma Gandhi all his life "*Vaiṣṇava jana to tene kahiye je pīr paraī jaṇe re*' (The true man of God is he, who identifies himself with the sufferings of others). It is not therefore just a matter of the difference between the vocation of a saint and the vocation of a poet emphasised in a statement like the one made by Yeats ('the saint goes straight to the centre, while the poet must return to the ring) After all, Narsi Mehta himself was a great saint as well as a great poet and there are so many others like him in the Bhakti Movement we have been discussing here. Moreover, what is called a *Bhakta* or a *Santa* in Indian tradition is not quite the same category which is designated as 'saint' in the Christian tradition. There are obvious similarities and obvious differences too which need not be elaborated here. One need not renounce the world in order to become a *bhakta* or a *bhakti* poet. What Tagore declares in one of his well-known songs in fact applies not only to himself but to many of the bhakti poets as well. "My liberation lies not in renouncing the world"—he says; "I long to taste freedom in the midst of all sorts of entanglements." Poets like Tukārāma and Narasī Mehtā would have readily accepted this. 'Only through time, time is conquered'—as T.S. Eliot has put it in one of his famous poems.' That indeed is the poet's way and that indeed has been the way of the poets from the Vedic times to medieval times and even down to our own modern times in some of the most significant practitioners of the art. Had not Kṛṣṇa himself told Arjuna: "I am Time, the all-destroyer?" Poetry at all times has had to confront and befriend this all-destroying time in order to be able to see through it. Poetry, in other words, has always been and shall always be a uniquely valuable means of contending with and removing the oppressive weight of time from this world of our experience. That is exactly where its birth and growth—its genesis as well as its process—appears to share a common ground with the experience of the *bhakta* and the mystic and even of some existential philosophers. Thus, as we meditate upon the central metaphor of the chariot and the charioteer in the *Kaṭhopaniṣad*, we find a sudden and quite unexpected illumination of the metaphor and its hidden meaning in Vedic poetry. Let me quote this verse from Atharvaveda:

> Time drives as a horse with seven reins, thousand-eyed, unageing, possessing much speed; him the inspired poets mount; his wheels are all beings. (XIX:53)

With this Vedic image of the inspired poet mounting the Pegasus of time, I would like to conclude this series of lectures on Indian Poetry and Poetics. I wish to thank you all, ladies and gentlemen, for accompanying me on this arduous journey through unfamiliar territory. I hope it was not such a tedium for you. For myself, it has been a most delightful and memorable occasion. I thank the trustees and the office-bearers of Temenos Academy for making it possible for me to come all the way from India to share my views with you. Above all, I am grateful to Dr. Kathleen Raine, without whose inspiration and initiative, these lectures would never have come into being at all. No ritual of thanksgiving, however sincere and fervent, can really measure upto an adequate acknowledgement of what I owe to her in terms of constant support and encouragement. Thank you once again, dear friends, for your gracious and most attentive presence through four memorable evenings. One hopes and prays with Shakespeare that what was after all, mere love's labour pure and simple, need not necessarily be lost; one simultaneously hopes and prays with a similar sentiment expressed by Kālidāsa in *Kumārasambhava*: *Kleśah phalena punarnavatām vidhatte.*[8]

---

8. Kālidāsa, Kumārasambhava, Canto V. The verses celebrate the happy reunion of Śiva and Pārvatī at the end of a long and painful series of austerities performed by Her. 'All's well that ends well' would be a close parallel to the meaning intended here.